THE REVIT® FORMULA

www.TheRevitFormula.com

Three Point Press

First Edition

Copyright © 2019 by Edgar E.B.
Published by Three Point Press
All rights reserved.

No part of this book may be reproduced or transmitted in any form or by any means, electronic or mechanical, including photo copying, recording, or by any information storage or retrieval system, without prior written permission from the publisher.

Limited Liability/ Disclaimer of Warranty

Every effort has been made to ensure that this book contains accurate and current information. The publisher and the author make no representations or warranties with respect to the accuracy or completeness of the contents of this work and specifically disclaim all warranties, including without limitation warranties of fitness for a particular purpose. No warranty may be created or extended by sales or promotional materials. The advise and strategies contained herein may not be suitable for every situation. This work is sold with the understanding that the publisher is not engaged in rendering legal, accounting, or other professional services. I professional assistance is required, the service of a competent professional person should be person should be sought. Neither the publisher nor the author shall be liable for damages arising herefrom. The fact that an organization or Website is referred to in this work as a citation and/or a potential source of further information does not mean that the author or the publisher endorses the information the organization or the Website may provide or recommendations it may make. Further, readers should be aware that Internet Websites listed in this work may have changed or disappeared between when this work was written and when it is read.

Trademarks

Autodesk and Revit are registered trademarks of Autodesk, Inc. All other trademarks are the property of their respective owners. Three Point Press and Edgar E.B., is not associated with any product or vendor mentioned in this book.

ISBN 978-1-7335976-0-9

Websites
www.therevitformula.com
www.threepointpress.com

THE REVIT® FORMULA

PARAMETERS AND FORMULAS

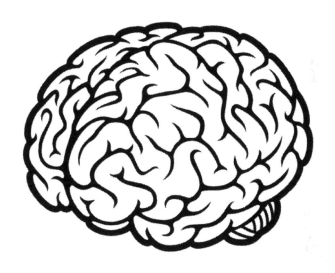

EDGAR E.B.

CONTENTS

PREFACE vi
INTRODUCTION x

1. PRE - PARAMETERS AND FORMULAS

LEGEND GUIDE 3
METAPHORS 5
UNITS 9
THE EDITOR 11
CREATING FAMILY TYPES 15

2. PARAMETERS

PARAMETERS - GENERAL 19
CREATING YOUR FIRST PARAMETER 21
PARAMETER PROPERTIES 22
INSTANCE VS. TYPE PARAMETER OPTION 27
FAMILY VS. SHARED PARAMETER OPTION 31
CREATING YOUR FIRST SHARED PARAMETER 33
ASSOCIATING PARAMETERS 37

3. FORMULAS

RECAP 43
ANATOMY OF A FORMULA 45
SIMPLE FORMULAS 47
COMPLEX FORMULAS 51

4. FORMULA IDEAS

ANATOMY OF A FORMULA PART DEUX — 63
PROXY PARAMETERS — 65
INSTANCE AND TYPE PARAMETER TRICK — 67
MAKE ANYTHING METRIC — 69
SUPPORT AND GRAYING OUT PARAMETERS — 73
HORIZONTAL OR VERTICAL FORMULAS? — 75
NEXT LEVEL FORMULA WIDTH WITH INTERVALS — 77
TEXT FORMULAS — 85

5. POST - PARAMETERS AND FORMULAS

PARAMETER ORGANIZING — 91
COMMON ERRORS — 97
TIPS AND TRICKS — 101
FINAL THOUGHTS — 103
CONTACT US — 104
DEDICATION — 105

PREFACE

I've been making families, for a leading interiors design firm in California for over 10 years, and in that time I learned that in Revit, families are king, and if families drive the Revit platform, then I would argue that family parameters and formulas drive Revit. If you can master these two things well; parameters and formulas, then the rest of the platform will be a walk in the park.

When I first embarked on the now enjoyable, back then stressful task of creating sleek, efficient, and lightweight formula driven families, I bought a 400+ page book on Revit. The three-author homage to the platform was way, **WAY** over my head at the time. I opened the book (3) or (4) times before committing it to retirement. Although the book was good, it just covered too much. To be honest, the book ended up being more discouraging than encouraging for a beginner.

So, years and countless obstacles resolved later, the idea for this book was born. This book would be **THE BOOK** I wished I had when I first started, when I was banging my head against my desk in frustration (true story) reading long-winded mechanical explanations of how parameters and formulas work. Pouring over countless scattered pages and pages of tutorials, blogs, and websites that although helpful, in my opinion, were written for people who already were familiar with parameters and formulas. People like me now, not people like me then.

This book is designed to have no fluff, no anecdotal stories to thicken up its pages in an attempt to command a higher price. This book is intended to be concise, affordable, and something you can carry, period.

The goal is, to cut through the dry, illegible, and bloated tutorials written by software Engineers, and provide an affordable, concentrated, pocketable, and utilitarian guide to parameters and formulas **written by a Designer for Designers**.

Let me reiterate this, **by a Designer for Designers**, you, the Architect, Interiors Designer, Structural, Electrical, MEP, the recently graduated, etc.

Now, before we dive in, let me give you a quick rundown of how I ended up in the position of making highly parametric formula driven families. However, before I do, let me be clear; this book is not about me. This book is intended and organized for you to go out and start implementing its content.

If you want to get going jump right into the introduction, otherwise, stick around. Perhaps you are where I was at the beginning. Maybe you have been tasked with overseeing a BIM library, to create new content, or you are **looking for a job**, newly out of College, and in need of furthering your skills. In any event, my story may help you double down on mastering your new talent, and hopefully, have the opposite effect the bible size book had on me when I was cluelessly looking for answers.

MY STORY.

When I first began, Revit was starting to become mainstream amongst large Architectural firms who started requiring that their sub-contractors work in Revit to stay competitive. I was hired straight out of College after obtaining my Bachelor of Architecture by a California Interiors design company a couple of years before the shift from CAD to Revit. My job was to oversee the production of Construction Documents for private and public Universities and research facilities all around the country and a few in Canada and overseas.

The job was demanding enough with the CAD tools the company had developed over the past 20 years, then overnight poof!, we are switching to Revit.

So, they did what all companies do, they signed us up for a one-week basic crash course in Revit, and sent us home with an Autodesk book half the size of the 400+ page one I already had. We still had no clue. The paradigm shift was just too big. I'd remind you no one had worked in 3D at the time unless it was for marketing. Eventually, we hired someone with experience and tasked him with developing new tools in Revit, like title blocks, templates, and of course Families.

For the next few months project started to pour in, and we started to get familiarized with the new platform. There was no time to angst about the shift; every day was about the deadline, although our new Revit expert did an excellent job of getting a working system up and running, which allowed the company to move forward, the increase in overtime was noticeable.

Worse than the deadlines and increase in production time, we started getting emails from clients complaining of floating fittings, sinks and base cabinets protruding through benchtops.

3D raised the client's expectations for our work. Now our work was not just producing Construction Documents, now it was that plus helping the client with their marketing efforts. Key to their marketing material, they now demanded more and more quality and realism from our models. We knew that we still had work to be done. I knew that there had to be a reason why Revit was taking off. There had to be a reason why the **WHOLE industry** moved in this direction. The reason I later understood was not just 3D, but 4D. Schedules, global oversight of complex models, and clash detection. The reason was **BIM**, in particular, the 'I' in BIM; Information.

So, what to do? I was happy to do my job and had very little interest in the development of content. Though, I quickly realized that if I wanted to have a 40-hour work week, I needed to fix this, and fix this now.

I began looking at our new library and concluded that if we were to go home on time, our library needed to be smarter, lighter, and prebuilt, e.g., a bench top that had a sink required a nested sink and fittings. This would cut down on time as opposed to dropping all three components separately. So, I began to develop a considerably more complex set of formula-driven-components with nested families that did just that. After a while, my components started to gain traction in the open market (the office), and I began to split my time 50/50 between CD's production and BIM management.

95% of the families used at the company were custom-made, simply put, they were tailored to work exactly as the demand for extreme turnarounds deemed it. In the years that followed, I designed and implemented, dozens and dozens of components, as well as developed the way that production worked within the company. Storing, managing projects, details, milestone archiving, etc.

The main issue that plagued the company's productivity was that it was impossible to know what was going on in elevation and 3D while you were in plan-view. Going back and forth meant loss of time. Drafter error or copying components from room to room would often result in base cabinets protruding through the bench top, or fittings floating above the bench top. The solution; **Colors**.

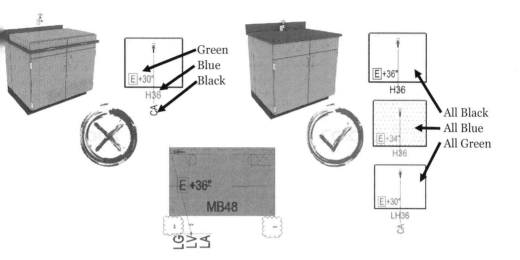

By using colors, we could color code labels, patterns and line work to match specific heights, e.g., black = 36", blue = 34" (ADA), and green = 30" (sitting height). With these three colors, we could know, with great confidence, the height of all components at a glance. If there is a green cabinet amongst a string of black ones, then you know the green is not the right height.

Another big issue was a growing number of types per component. One family could harbor 20 or 30 types, confusing the user and causing delays. Through formulas, we programmed a pull, as shown in the lit MB48 above to change width at 6" increments and stop at a specific width. We did the same to the components heights and virtually eliminated all types. These formulas are in the book. **Hint**.

While there were many hurdles more, these two were paramount to efficiency, and productivity, and allowed the company to tackle larger and larger projects throughout the years. Additionally, in terms of growth, I always felt that I was more than a step ahead of my coworkers regarding BIM for merely knowing how Revit works, from the inside out.

I strongly advise you stick with this book or at least keep it close, it will help you get out of annoying errors, and guide you out of rookies mistakes. Take it from someone who did them all. If you have this in your hands, you're already miles ahead of where I started. I commend you for your initiative. Learn, share, and be prosperous, plus **get your boss to pay for it**. It is a tax-deductible expense ;)

Edgar E.B.
NCARB

INTRODUCTION

First some layout metrics; this book has been organized in (5) parts. On both ends of the book, you have the content you need before, and after you learn parameters and formulas. In the middle, you have parameters, formulas, and some formula ideas. It's that simple.

Now, while the main focus of this book is to learn parameters and formulas in an un-intimidating format, and this is the primary goal, there is a secondary goal... STEAL! Well not really since you did purchase the book, It's more like COPY!

There are very useful tried and tested formulas, and formula combinations in this book, that can **help anyone**. So, if you don't have time to digest all of its content, simply copy some examples and learn that way too. There is no wrong way; the point is to learn.

Learn either by going step by step, by trial and error, or by copying and backward engineering formulas later. **JUST LEARN**. You'll be surprised that at some point it actually becomes fun. You will quickly notice that you begin to see things that your coworkers don't.

Furthermore, you will begin to think of modeling differently. You will find solutions to problems by thinking, "I can write a formula to solve that." That moment is the **aha moment**. Enjoy, grow and succeed.

Oh, and if you bought a digital copy of the book, great! Though I highly recommend you keep a pocketable hardcopy version **on your desk** for reference. Enjoy.

Edgar E.B.
NCARB

INTENTIONAL BREAK

PART 1

MORE OF A 'THINGS TO KNOW' BEFORE YOU JUMP
INTO PARAMETERS AND FORMULAS. SOME BASIC
SETUPS; AN OVERVIEW IN PREPARATION FOR THE
MAIN EVENT.

PRE-PARAMETERS AND FORMULAS

LEGEND GUIDE

We'll need to sort through a bit of data throughout the book. Hopefully in a graphical manner that doesn't seem daunting. Below is a series of symbols that were developed with this in mind. While we'll be thorough at every step of the way and note what each symbol means when in doubt come to this sheet for a quick reference refresher.

(TR) TRIGGER PARAMETER

Symbol used to identify the trigger parameter or parameters. These parameters are the ones you activate, modify, the ones that set the formula in motion.

(OT) OUTPUT PARAMETER

Symbol used to identify the parameter where the final formula is being used. This parameter is usually grayed out, and its formula is fed commands by the trigger parameters and the support parameters. This parameter is always connected to an extrusion, visibility, or the dimension that stretched the family in the case of a Length parameter.

(SP) SUPPORT PARAMETER

Symbol used to identify the parameters that help the output parameter get its job done. Let's just say that if the output parameter is **Elvis**, then the support parameters are the **roadies** that do all the heavy lifting behind the scenes.

(R) RESULTS

Symbol used to highlight a result after a lengthy explanation

(?) QUESTION MARK

Symbol used to highlight an unknown.

(1) NUMBERS

Symbol used to highlight a specific sequential process.

(A) LETTERS

Symbol used to organize paragraphs in no particular sequence.

e.g. = For example.

INTENTIONAL BREAK

METAPHORS

I have always liked metaphors to explain complex concepts. Metaphors provide a more visual description of a concept, word, or thought that can be hard to explain otherwise.

Below is a list of (3) of my favorite Revit metaphors which have helped, and continue to help me visualize Revit concepts in relation to learning.

They may become more useful as you approach each topic, but merely being exposed to them, upfront can help you grasp the topics better as you reach each one.

1 THE BODY

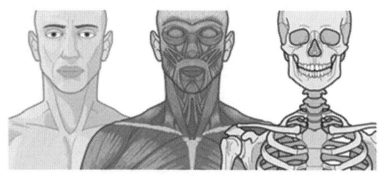

The body metaphor refers to the way families are built. Similar to the body, families have bones, muscle, and skin. In Revit families reference planes are bones, parameters are muscle, and geometry is skin.

Out of these (3) systems, believe it or not, the geometry is **not** the most critical system. Getting the reference planes to move accurately with the parameters is the most vital part. Once you get the bones and muscles to flex without **errors** then adding geometry is easy. In fact, sometimes you can reuse the bones and muscle and create an entirely different looking family.

The final element is the brain (formulas). While formulas really push your families to an entirely new level of functionality, formulas can be added at any time, even at the end.

Half or more of the book is dedicated to this important topic, see the next page for further illustrations on the relation between the body and families.

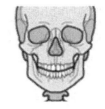

REFEREANCE PLANES & LINES (BONES)

 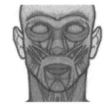

PARAMETERS (MUSCLE)

SOLIDS AND VOIDS - GEOMETRY (SKIN)

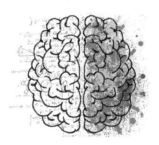

FORMULAS (BRAIN)

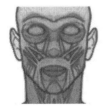 &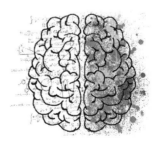

THIS BOOK IS ALL ABOUT THE...

A FEW TIPS ON MODELING

Although still on the analogy section, the body metaphor is a direct metaphor for modeling. See below a few tips on the topic.

Make as many reference planes as you want, go crazy, just make sure of (2) things:

1. **LABEL ALL YOUR REFERENCE PLANES**

    I wish someone had told me you could name reference planes at the beginning. Naming your **bones** helps identify and keep order over the multiple RP's you've made and for what purpose they were made. Additionally, it lets you move extrusions between the reference planes using the **edit work plane** button (see below, right). Once clicked you get a list of all your RP's and you can move geometry, lines, and embedded families between them, a super valuable function.

2. **SET MOST REFERENCE PLANES TO BE NOT A REFERENCE**

    If not, when you hover over your finished model with the align tool, all the reference planes will light up making your family confusing and dirty. You should only have 6 reference planes set as references. The 4 perimeter ones, and the 2 center ones.

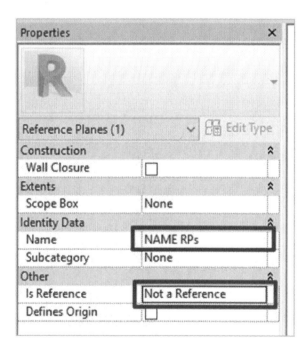

② THE COMPUTER VIRUS

The computer virus metaphor refers to the way formulas operate. Like a computer virus, the formulas you write are always dormant until something "**triggers**" them, similarly as when you download an infected file to your computer. The computer is not infected until you press the .exe file and set the virus in motion, the same is true with formulas.

③ THE IOS

The IOS metaphor refers to the way YOU build families.

The IOS operating system is famous for its elegance and simplicity. Contrary to it's Linux and Windows counterparts, where a user can be overwhelmed by customizable options and access to the backend of the system. IOS hides from the end user the day to day operations of the system and offers a hiccup-free experience for which it's famous for.

When making highly parametric families, the same mentality applies. You can use formulas and parameters to restrict, **control**, and minimize mistakes. In essence, you become the IOS programmer, and you must anticipate mistakes. You will be the author of the complex backend, and offer the end user an incredibly simple set of controls on the front end per your design.

UNITS

Before anything, it is always important to set your units. This is particularly important in the creation of formulas where 2x3 can be 2x3 inches or 2x3 feet.

UNITS AND SCALE

Units are synonymous with scale (which I also recommend setting upfront), e.g., if I am modeling furniture, anything smaller than 60" to 72", I recommend staying with inches. Furniture is usually dimensioned in inches in most industries, anything larger should be in feet, e.g., a crane, a car, or another big piece of equipment.

Now, in terms of scale, I always recommend working in the scale in which the model will be used. If your model is intended to be used in enlarged plans, then I would set the scale at 1/4", if the model will be used in overall plans, then I would set the scale at 1/8". This is important because you may need to change text and dimension scales in your family to work comfortably or find a text and dimension scale that works for both scales.

These are things to consider when building your family templates, for now, concerning formulas, we really just need to pick units, since it will affect your thought process later down the road. I prefer and recommend inches (not the default) since most families are small.

A note on units, when changed, they only affect the current Revit model, not the entire system. This means you can have some families set to inches, and some set to feet within the family editor. Same goes for the overall project's environment, not just families.

SETTING UP UNITS

To set up units, merely type **UN** on your keyboard to summon the **Project units** interface. Alternately, under the manage tab, click on the Project Units icon.

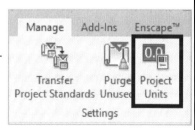

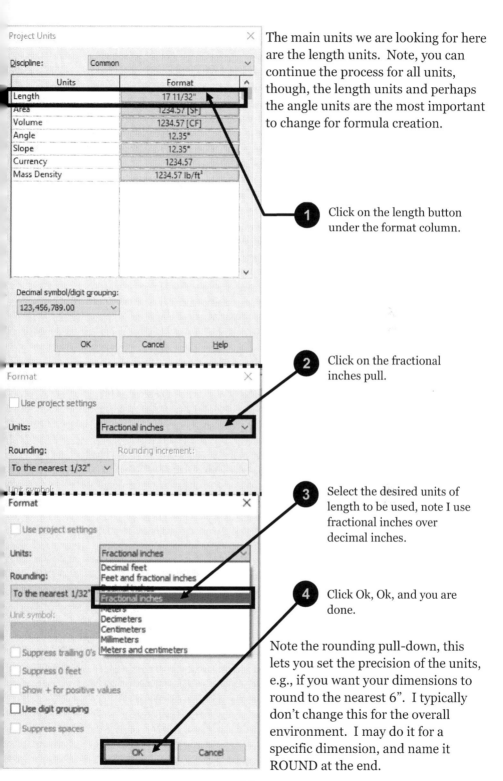

The main units we are looking for here are the length units. Note, you can continue the process for all units, though, the length units and perhaps the angle units are the most important to change for formula creation.

1. Click on the length button under the format column.

2. Click on the fractional inches pull.

3. Select the desired units of length to be used, note I use fractional inches over decimal inches.

4. Click Ok, Ok, and you are done.

Note the rounding pull-down, this lets you set the precision of the units, e.g., if you want your dimensions to round to the nearest 6". I typically don't change this for the overall environment. I may do it for a specific dimension, and name it ROUND at the end.

THE EDITOR

Akin to a computer programmer's console, the family types editor is where all parameters, types, and formulas are created, it is essential to be comfortable with this environment.

When creating a simple family, you typically begin with three parameters WIDTH, DEPTH, and HEIGHT. These parameters are made in the family types editor. If you are familiar with creating simple families, then you may already be familiar with the editor, but when making highly parametric families, you will spend considerably more time on this screen (because you want to, not have to). See below example of the editor in full use with more than a dozen parameters, and formulas.

Parameter	Value	Formula
Constraints		
LASER_CURTAIN	☐	=
CURTAIN (default)	☑	=
ANGLE_FLIP (default)	☐	=
ANGLE (default)	0.00°	=
Text		
KEYNOTE	TBD	=
Materials and Finishes		
MATERIAL	TOEKICK	=
Dimensions		
WIDTH (default)	60"	=
SKIRT_HEIGHT	12"	=
RADIUS	12"	=
DEPTH	2"	=
CURTAIN_THICKNESS	1/4"	=
CEILING_HEIGHT	108"	=
Analysis Results		
STRAIGHT_SKIRT_VIS (default)	☑	= not(ANGLE > 0°)
SKIRT_HEIGHT_USED	-12"	= SKIRT_HEIGHT * FLIP
LASER_CURTAIN_USED (default)	☐	= if(not(CURTAIN), OFF, LASER_CURTAIN)
BLACKOUT_CURTAIN (default)	☑	= if(not(CURTAIN), OFF, not(LASER_CURTAIN))
ANGLE_USED (default)	90.00°	= if(ANGLE > 0°, ANGLE, 90°)
ANGLE2_VIS (default)	☐	= and(ANGLE > 0°, not(ANGLE_FLIP))
ANGLE1_VIS (default)	☐	= and(ANGLE > 0°, ANGLE_FLIP)
Other		
ON	☑	= 0 + 0 = 0
OFF	☐	= 0 + 0 = 1
FLIP	-1.000000	= -1

THE EDITOR OVERVIEW - BUTTONS

Bellow is an overview of the different functions used to create parameters and family types. Parameters are used to create formulas, to access the family editor go to the **create** ribbon and press the **family types** symbol.

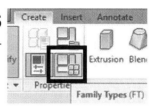

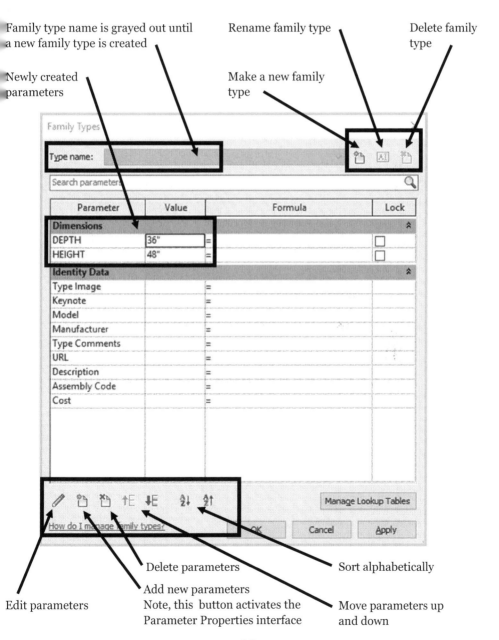

THE EDITOR OVERVIEW - FIELDS

Below is an overview of all the different fields, columns, and rows in the family types editor.

(A) TYPE NAME
The Inactive drop-down menu which becomes active once one or more types are created. Once you have multiple family types, this drop-down box lets you change between family types, and alter the type's values.

(B) SEARCH PARAMETERS BOX
Is a typical search box. Very helpful in highly parametric families once they start getting out of hand (which is not a bad thing).

(C) PARAMETER COLUMN
The parameter column is where all your new parameters are listed.

(D) PARAMETER GROUPS (BLUE ROWS)
These blue groups help you lump your parameters into **chunks** for better readability. Note Revit has pre-selectively organizing fields for each parameter, e.g., **Dimensions** for Length parameters, **Text** and **Materials** are organized under the same name. Some are not predetermined, and Revit will lump them under the **Other** group. In any event, you have control to assign you parameters groups as you see fit. I recommend reading the 'Parameters organizing' section under the 'Post - parameters and formulas' Part for a full explanation, and ideas.

(E) VALUE COLUMN
Here is where the value for the parameter is given, e.g., on or off for a Y/N parameter, or a specific Length for Length parameters.

(F) FORMULA COLUMN
This is the area where formulas are written, see an example on the next page for WIDTH.

(G) LOCK COLUMN
I typically ignore these locks. What these locks do, is to restrict or allow altering the parameter values outside of the family types editor. Let me elaborate.

If locked, and you intend to change, e.g., WIDTH outside the types editor (in plan view), by just changing the dimension you will get an error warning. If unlocked, you would be altering the parameter's WIDTH as you wish without ever entering the editor. Again, I choose not to fiddle with this.

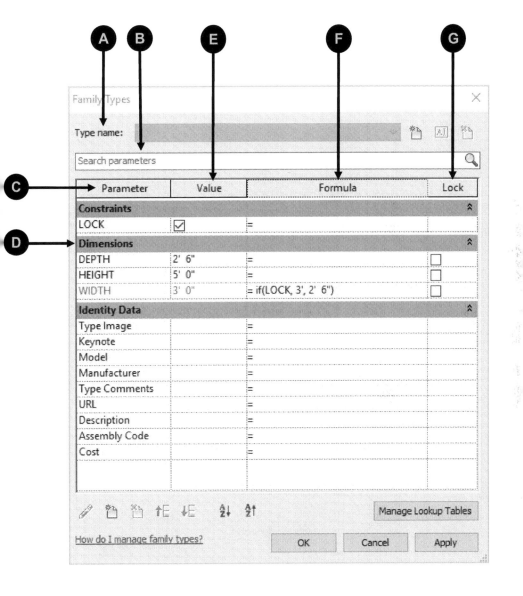

CREATING FAMILY TYPES

While not a huge fan of family types, 95% of changes to families are done through types. I go out of my way to create elaborate formulas to eliminate types, but types are the norm, in Revit.

Family types are all the custom variations you make within a family. Let's say you have a family named MT (for movable table). You may need dozens of types for each variation of the MT, e.g., MT6030, MT5430, MT4830, etc., etc. And that is just the WIDTH, add the DEPTH changes, and you get an idea of how long types can get. The question is, how are they created? Well, within the family types editor. See below steps for creating a basic Length type.

1. From within the editor, Click on the new type button.

2. A name box appears, change the default name to whatever you want. Here I am naming my type MT6030, click OK.

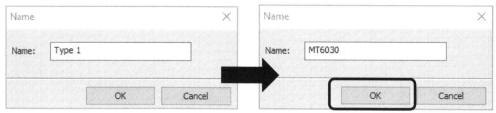

3. The grayed out type name: field becomes MT6030.

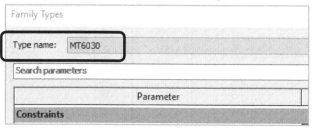

4. Don't forget, you still need to change the WIDTH, and DEPTH Length parameters to match your new type name.

5. Wash, rinse, repeat, and you get a nice list of types.

INTENTIONAL BREAK

PART 2

THE MUSCLE IN REVIT. EVERYTHING YOU NEED TO KNOW ON PARAMETERS FOR SCHEDULING AND FORMULA CREATION.

PARAMETERS

PARAMETERS - GENERAL

The **muscle** in Revit. Parameters either move something, make something visible or not, change a Label/ Text, change materials, etc., etc. Parameters make the difference between something that just looks good and something that **is** good. Parameters make families functional, schedulable, and intuitive, hence the name **parametric** families.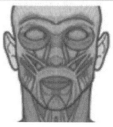

You can make a family without parameters, in fact, many sophisticated company-manufactured families often **look good, but <u>are no-good</u>**. Many times these families are created in Solidworks and then dropped into the Revit family editor.

The reality is, if you need a static family, these work, the problem is, when you need a dynamic/ parametric family, these do not work. Changes to dimensions, materials, schedulability, and sortability are paramount to the "I" in BIM; information. With no parameters to communicate the information, families at best become limited, at worst become useless. This is where your custom family creating skills overshadows that of the manufacturers; by adding the 'I' in BIM, you the builder don't just gain new families, you gain **control**. Control over Revit, and control over the information you are already inputting into your model as you model along. This is 4D, this is the true power of the platform; **information**, and it all begins with parameters.

FORMULABLE PARAMETERS

Not all parameters are **Formulable.** Since we are focusing on learning the creation of formulas, it is essential to know this up front. For example, you cannot use the **material** parameter in a formula, or use formulas in the material parameter itself, even though it has a formula field in front of it.

Non-formulable parameters can still be used in schedules and are highly valuable, but there is no need to plan complex formula setups for these parameters only to realize after hours that you couldn't use them in the first place.

A good rule of thumb is, if the parameter is number-based then you can use it in formulas. That said, there is a couple of non-number based **formulable** parameters. The **YES/NO** parameter, and the **Text** parameter. The text parameter can be tricky to use though, quotation symbols need to encase the text when making text formulas but don't worry about the details now, there is a whole section that touches base on text parameters. For now, just know that **Text** and **Y/N** parameters are the few non-number based parameters that can be used in formulas.

NAMING PARAMETERS

Before anything, it is essential to know how to name your parameters. Below is a list of dos and don'ts for you to consider. Ultimately picking a naming strategy is entirely up to you, and should be something you are comfortable with, or something that makes sense to you.

- Revit parameters are case sensitive, meaning, the parameter Width is an entirely different parameter than the parameters WIDTH or WidtH.
- Do not use dashes like WIDTH-FRONT, or WIDTH-BACK. Revit can interpret the dash as a minus sign later in formulas, instead use an underscore for a similar effect, e.g., WIDTH_FRONT or WIDTH_BACK.
- In general stay away from special characters in your naming, e.g., \,:,{,},[,], etc.
- Consider not using spaces between words. Instead, use underscores, this will cut down on doubts like **if** you used spaces or not, or mistakes like accidentally using too many spaces between words.
- Consider using all caps. Having your parameters in all capitals will help your custom parameters stand out from the default ones used by Revit. This helps you quickly identify your parameters in schedules vs. system parameters. An additional benefit is that you eliminate the case sensitivity in naming parameters.
- Avoid using numbers in your naming. Instead of WIDTH_1 or WIDTH_2, try WIDTH_A or WIDTH_B. This again helps when you are writing formulas clearly separate a parameter name from just length and integer numbers. That said, you can use them like 120V_VISIBILITY for an outlet. Avoid numbers, but if it makes sense to you, use them, this is not a rule, it is a suggestion.

HERE ARE SOME ADDITIONAL PERSONAL PREFERENCES.

- Be descriptive when making parameters, but keep it short.
- If you have many parameters that deal with the same element like labels; preface the parameters with LABELS, so they group together, e.g., LABEL_CUSTOM, LABEL_INSIDE, LABEL_ROTATE, LABEL_VISIBILITY, etc.
- Avoid excessive abbreviating. Let's say you have parameters that are named WIDTH_LOW and WIDTH_HIGH, and you want to shorten them to WI_LOW and WI_HIGH. If you can remember what WI means (3) years from now, go for it, if not, don't. These short sided abbreviations can cost you more grief and time later when trying to figure out what they meant, rather than just writing the whole thing out. Get used to longer formulas; again unless you can create a system that works for you.

CREATING YOUR FIRST PARAMETER

1 Open the family editor as we did in the previous section by going to the **create** tab, then **family types**.

2 Press the add new parameter button on the bottom left (second icon from the left), The parameter properties box will open.

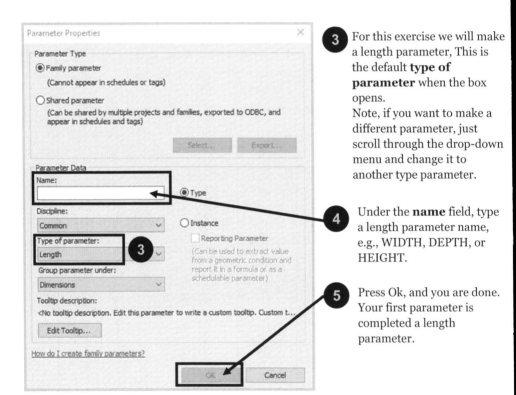

3 For this exercise we will make a length parameter, This is the default **type of parameter** when the box opens.
Note, if you want to make a different parameter, just scroll through the drop-down menu and change it to another type parameter.

4 Under the **name** field, type a length parameter name, e.g., WIDTH, DEPTH, or HEIGHT.

5 Press Ok, and you are done. Your first parameter is completed a length parameter.

Note all the different selections on the Parameter Properties box. On the next few pages, we will break down all the fields in detail.

PARAMETERS PROPERTIES

For the most part, creating a parameter is as easy as 1 through 5 (as noted on the previous sheet). Once you know what you are doing, you'll be making parameters in seconds, especially when you already know how many parameters you need, the type of parameters they will be, and what you are going to name your parameters.

For the most part, the parameter overview fields and options are pretty straightforward, except for two:

1. The Family parameter vs. the Shared parameter option.

2. The Type vs. Instance parameter option.

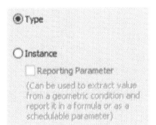

In my experience, these two fields trump most creators and end users at the beginning. For that reason we will break down the overview in two sections:

1. A simple pass with a brief description of all fields.

2. A detailed pass where we will circle back to these two fields for a more detailed explanation. **Just know this**, you do **NOT** need to get this right away. For the sake of making formulas, you can skip and move forward, but it's always a good idea to be exposed to tricky topics upfront, so when confronted with them and confusion sets in, you remember this was discussed before and can circle back for a refresher review.

PARAMETER PROPERTIES OVERVIEW (SIMPLE PASS)

Bellow is an overview of the different functions used to create parameters.

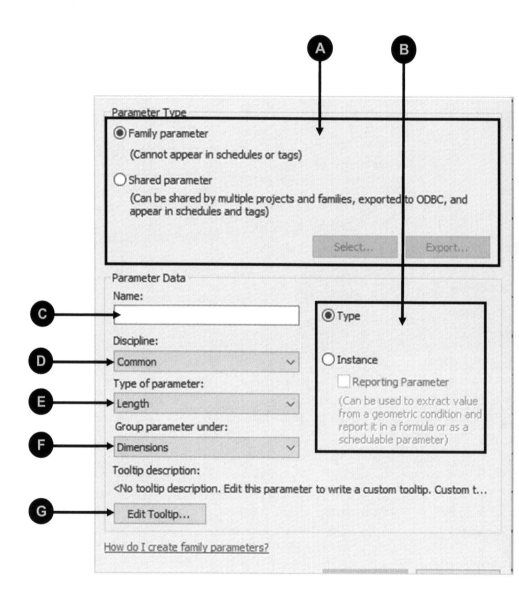

FAMILY OR SHARED PARAMETER OPTION
The family parameter option is selected by default, this option will create parameters that will not appear in any schedule once loaded in your project. For formula creation, most of your parameters will be this type.
The shared parameter option is used for scheduling purposes. When you create a parameter with this option, the parameter will appear in your project's schedules. This paramount for the 'I' in BIM. We will go into great detail on these options later.

TYPE OR INSTANCE PARAMETER OPTION
The type parameter option creates a parameter which is stronger than the instance parameter option. This parameter when altered affects every family in a project. Changes to type parameters are made within the family through the **edit type** button.
The instance parameter option will create a weaker parameter that when altered, it only affects one family in the project, the one you made the change to. This option will appear outside the family in the **properties** pane, instance parameter changes are made more on the fly. We will go into great detail on these two options later.

NAME
Here is where you name your parameter, e.g., a Length parameter could be named WIDTH, DEPTH, HEIGHT, etc.

DISCIPLINE
Use this pull-down to select the discipline that most closely represents your industry, what you choose here will alter the next selection list (Type of parameter).
This list is preset by Revit and is not alterable.

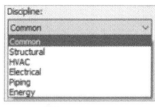

TYPE OF PARAMETER
This list is where you select the parameter type you need, e.g., a Length parameter, Number parameter, Y/N parameter, etc. This list is affected by the previous discipline selection. For example, you will not find HVAC parameters in the structural discipline.

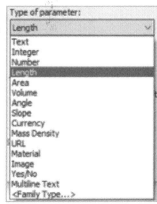

F **GROUP PARAMETERS UNDER**
This list groups your parameters. This represents the blue row on the family editor (letter 'D' on the Editor overview). For the most part, Revit does a pretty good job at automatically selecting this for you, e.g., a Length parameter is automatically put under the Dimensions section without you having to assign it. If you wish to be proactive, you can further sort your parameters to fit your needs.

See below example blue group header row for Dimensions.

G **EDIT TOOLTIP**
Although barely used, this tool is actually very helpful. This tool allows you to add a message for the end user explaining what your parameter will do. For some parameters this may not matter, e.g., HEIGHT might be clear enough that you may not need to explain, but what if you had a parameter named HEIGHT_B, you could add a message describing the difference between the two, when the user hovers over HEIGHT_B, your message will display. You may only end up using this tool a couple of times per family, but it can be very beneficial once you develop highly parametric families that have confusing, but necessary parameters that need clarification. It is a way to talk to the end user without actually talking to the end user.

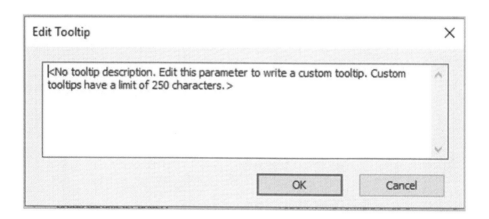

PARAMETER PROPERTIES OVERVIEW (DETAILED PASS)

As noted earlier, there are two options when making parameters that stump most beginner modelers, and end users:

1. The Family parameter vs. the Shared parameter option.

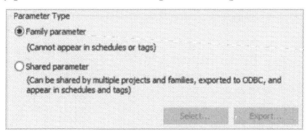

2. The Type parameter vs. Instance parameter option.

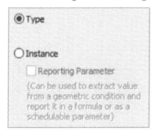

Lets review both in the next (2) sections. We will begin with Type vs. Instance parameters, since it is the most straightforward concept of the two, and finalize with the Parameter vs. Shared parameter option since this explanation requires us to make a shared parameter, which has its own challenges.

While both concepts are essential, for the sake of learning how to make formulas, they can just be left on their respective defaults (as shown above), and you can continue, but when ready to kick it up a notch, come back and re-read this section, since it will help you create a much more powerful system for your office.

INSTANCE VS. TYPE PARAMETERS OPTION

INSTANCE PARAMETERS

Instance parameters distinct behavior is:

1. They affect only (1) family type at a time.

2. All the parameters live **outside** the family.

Let's illustrate. Let's say you have a project with (3) movable tables. The WIDTH parameter for this table is an instance parameter. See below and on the next page for steps to change the WIDTH, and the outcome effect on all types on the project with an instance parameter.

① SELECT ONE OF YOUR FAMILIES
Note the properties pane change from floor plan properties to family properties.

② CHANGE THE PARAMETER VALUE
Scroll down through the family properties and look for your parameter. In this case, since it is a length parameter, it will be located under dimensions, we will change the CSTM_WIDTH parameter from 36" to 60".

③ NOTE THE BEHAVIOR
Out of the (3) families in the project, only (1) family was affected, the one you selected, the reason for this is that the parameter will just change the behavior for only (1) **instance** in the project, not all the types throughout the project. So, you could say the harm if an accidental change were to happen is minimal vs. a type parameter change, which is global.

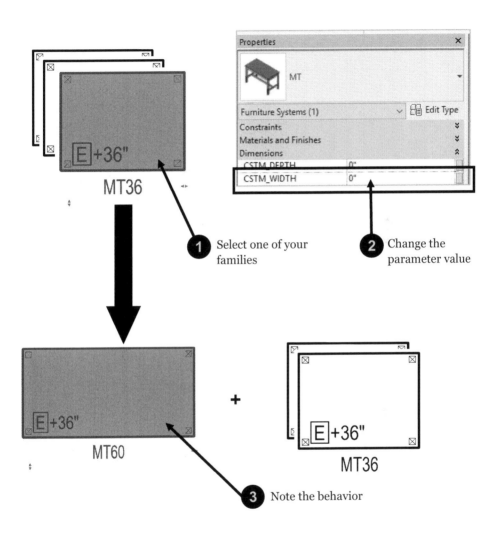

TYPE PARAMETERS
type parameters distinct behavior is:

1. They affect **ALL** family types of the altered type throughout the project.

2. All the parameters live **inside** the family.

Let's illustrate. Le'ts say you have a project with (3) movable tables. The WIDTH parameter for this table is a type parameter. See below and on the next page for steps to change the WIDTH, and the outcome effect on all types on the project with a type parameter.

Note to access the type parameters (inside) there is an extra step you will not find when altering an instance parameter.

❶ SELECT ONE OF YOUR FAMILIES
Note the properties pane change from floor plan properties to family properties.

❷ SELECT EDIT TYPE
This is the extra step you do not do on instance parameters. This steps grants you access to the inside of the family.

❸ CHANGE THE PARAMETER VALUE
Scroll down through the family properties and look for your parameter. In this case, since it is a length parameter, it will be located under dimensions, we would change the DEFLT_WIDTH parameter from 36" to 60".

❹ PRESS OK
Confirm changes.

❺ NOTE THE BEHAVIOR
All (3) families were affected, the reason for this is that the parameter changed **ALL** the behavior of the types in the project, not just one. So, you could say the harm if an accidental change were to happen is more severe vs. an instance parameter change, which only affects (1) type, this change is global.

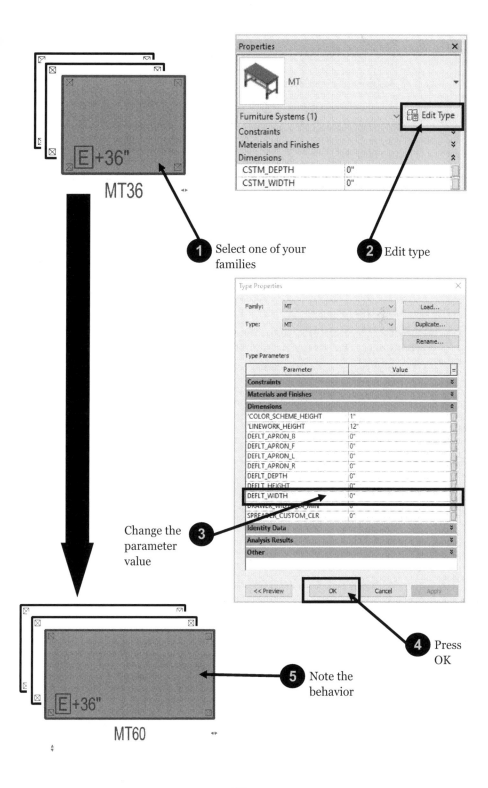

FAMILY VS. SHARED PARAMETER OPTION

FAMILY PARAMETERS

The family parameter option which **cannot** appear in schedules or tags, is **THE** option you will use 95% of the time, why? Because you do not need to schedule every parameter you make.

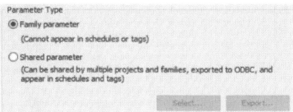

You will schedule WIDTH, DEPTH, HEIGHT, and maybe some features, like LOCKS, CASTERS, or other things you need to keep track of. Most families you really only need to schedule 4 or 5 parameters at a time, but you will make dozens of non-scheduled parameters. These parameters are the ones you make for **formulas.** These parameters are the ones you make for small changes like a benchtop's overhang, or the height of a backsplash. Just general items.

SHARED PARAMETERS

These parameters are targeted and schedulable. When you make Shared parameters, you essentially create a **database** of parameters you can export, insert, and **reuse**. This database is housed in a **.txt** file you will save somewhere on your computer or network. By **reuse**, I mean that once the database of parameters is made, you can insert parameters to other families, so you really end up making these once and reusing them forever. Shared parameters have (2) primary uses:

1. To make any parameter appear in schedules. Let's say you want to keep track of all benchtop's backsplash heights. You merely create a Shared parameter called BACKSPLASH_HEIGHT and apply it to the backsplash. This parameter now will appear in your project schedules moving forward.

2. For tags. If you make a Text parameter and you want to extract the information later in the project via a tag or keynote, the parameter needs to be a shared parameter so that the tag or keynote can connect to the text parameter. The tag will need to be connected to the same shared parameter as the one in your family via the shared parameter database (.txt file).

Out of these two options, for the most part, you will be making schedulable parameters. Let's go through the steps in creating shared parameters in the next section.

INTENTIONAL BREAK

CREATING YOUR FIRST SHARED PARAMETER

This section is tricky. Just know that mastering shared parameters is not easy, so stick with it, and practice. What makes this section difficult is the sheer number of steps. Try it out yourself more than once. It's just one of those things that require some practice.

1 WHEN YOU SELECT SHARED PARAMETER
Note the changes when you just select the shared parameter button. All parameter fields gray out (except for type and instance). This is because from here on all these fields will populate by the database you will create. This data once built, will populate itself.

2 CLICK SELECT
Click select to begin your first shared parameter database (fancy for a list of reusable parameters).

3 FIRST SCREEN
The first time you begin your shared parameters this screen can be confusing since it is completely empty. The reason is, you haven't yet made a parameter group and a parameter. So why do you need a parameter group and a parameter? Because when creating your shared parameters, shared parameters can be lumped by a group for organizing purposes. So, I can lump all my length parameters under a LENGTH_PARAMETERS group and have dozens of Length parameters under this group (which we will do shortly). I can make another group for TEXT_PARAMETERS, and use that just for text as well.

4 CLICK EDIT
The reason it is called edit is that once you create your first database (.txt file), every time you come back to add more parameters or groups, you will be editing the list. The first time is weird and confusing because it is empty and there is no direction.

5 CLICK CREATE
Since this is your first database (txt. File), you are clicking **Create**, if you already had created a .txt file, then you would click **Browse** to steal some previously created parameters or to add parameters to an existing list.

6 LOCATE WHERE YOUR .TXT FILE WILL LIVE
Now you have a windows screen prompting you for a name and location where your database (.txt file) will live. Find an appropriate folder on your computer or network, name the file, and click save.

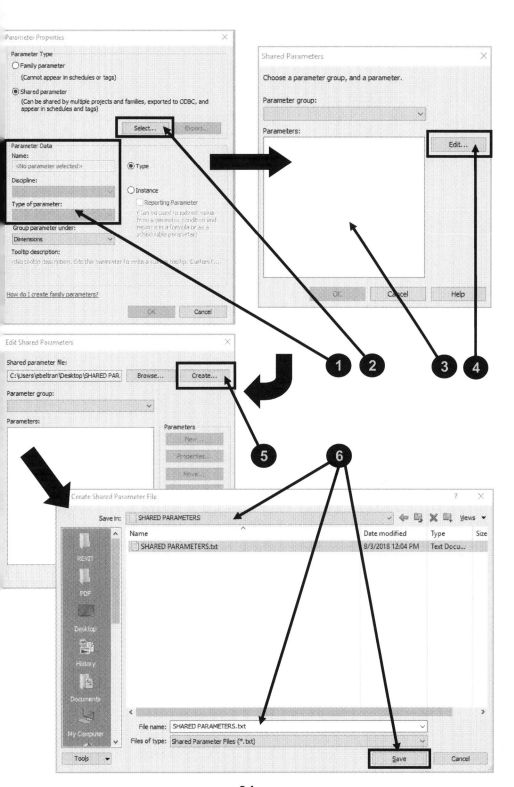

SHARED PARAMETERS (CONTINUED)

7. NAME / CREATE YOUR GROUP
Once you set up your database (txt. file), you'll be prompted for a group name. This group name is where you'll bundle up your shared parameters. See example for LENGTH_PARAMERS group. Under this group, I can place all Length/ Dimension parameters which will make it easy to find in the future vs. having them all jumbled up with Y/N, Integer parameters, etc. Finalize, press OK.

8. MAKE YOUR PARAMETER
Note this window. This window is the basic properties for making a parameter (as previously discussed). The reason the parameter fields are grayed out back in step 1, is because the fields will be filled in by this step. In the future, you will pretty much start at this step, if you are just adding to an existing group. Finalize, press OK.

9. BACK TO THE SECOND SCREEN (STEP 5)
Note this screen. You are back in step 5, except this time it's not blank, and the fields make sense. It is easy now to see and understand how parameters are grouped. Now from this screen you can create more groups and add more parameters. I added a couple more parameters so that the parameter section makes sense graphically. Finalize, press OK.

10. BACK TO FIRST SCREEN (STEP 3)
When you are back to this screen it feels like you may have made a mistake since it looks so much like the screen in step 9, it is not. In the future, once you have the groups and parameters you need, you will not need to go further from this screen. You will just come here and select from the premade list of parameters and groups. **If** you need more, then you would press edit again and repeat step 9. Select the parameter you need, press OK.

11. DONE
Look at the Parameter Data now, it is all grayed out and prefilled with the information from the .txt file. The only remaining options you have is if you want to change the Group parameter under option (which you do not have to and can accept the default) and if you want your parameter to be instance vs. type (look back at the previous section for the difference between the two). You are done, Finalize, press OK.

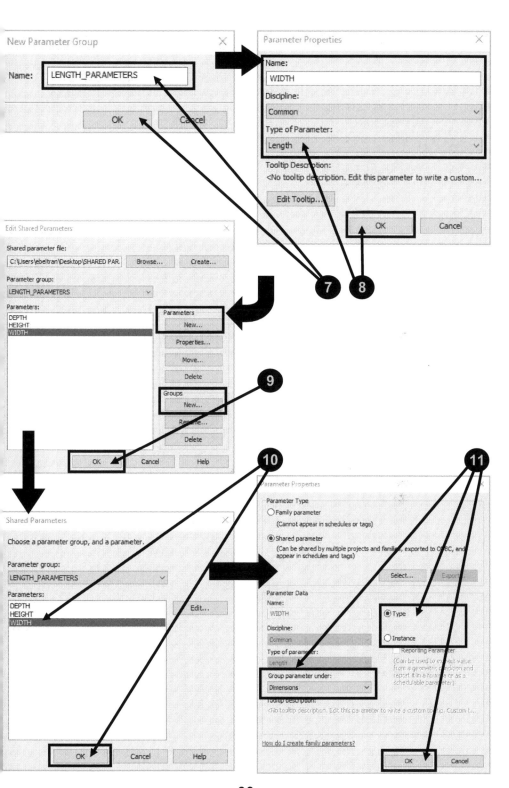

ASSOCIATING PARAMETERS

So, now you can make all sorts of parameters, what do we do with these parameters? Well, it is time to learn how to associate parameters with the family. All the parameters you deem to be **output**/ connect to Dimensions, geometry, or materials need to be connected. Let's go through some essential elements and how they connect.

LENGTH PARAMETERS

1. Select your dimension.
2. The modify tab will light up, and a Label pull-down will appear.
3. Pull on the label, and select the Length parameter to be associated with the dimension.
4. Now the dimension should read the same as the parameter. At this point, flex your parameter, and the dimension will move your reference planes.

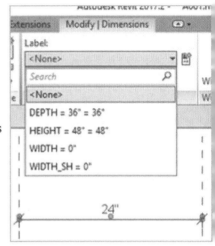

Y/N PARAMETERS

You can associate Y/N parameters to geometry, embedded families, labels, lines, etc. What you are looking for is this: In the properties pane for the element, you are associating. Simply:

1. Touch the element (geometry, label, line, etc.)
2. Click on the square as noted above.
3. A list of Y/N parameters will pop-up.
4. Select the parameter you will associate.
5. Press ok, and done.

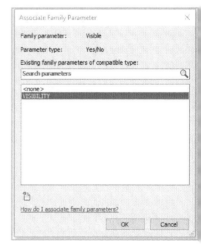

MATERIAL PARAMETERS

Materials are applied to geometry. The whole process is very similar to the Y/N parameter. What you are looking for is this:

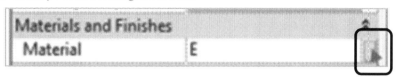

In the properties pane for the element, you are associating. Simply:
1. Touch the element (geometry)
2. Click on the square as noted above.
3. A list of material parameters will pop-up.
4. Select the parameter you will associate.
5. Press ok, and done.

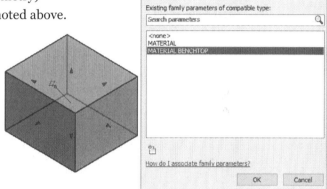

Note that when associating materials there are (2) ways to do this.
1. Is the method above, where you are associating the material to a parameter, and then the material can be altered in the project, so the geometry becomes wood, metal, glass, etc., and you can alter at will.
2. Is where you apply the material to the geometry directly, not through a parameter. In this case, you are applying the material permanently, and it will not be alterable later in the project. I prefer the first method's flexibility, but I can see the second as a way to minimize material parameters. Let's illustrate.

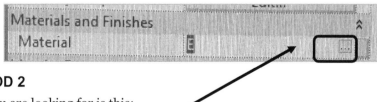

METHOD 2

What you are looking for is this:
The second square with (3) dots to the left of the previously used square. It is initially invisible. To make it visible merely click in the empty space between Material and the old square, here.
Similarly as before, follow these steps:

1. Touch the element (geometry)
2. Click on the square as noted above
3. A list of materials will pop-up. This is the same list that would pop-up if you were selecting the material through the materials parameter. Select one, and it will be associated with the geometry, but not to a parameter.

Note: when selecting a material, via a parameter, this method, or in the project, you **do not** need to go to the material browser shown here. If you know the materials name, you can just type it in. This is the reason I like my materials to be **SUPER SIMPLE**, e.g., E = Epoxy, or W=Wood. Or two letters, EP = Epoxy, WO = Wood. It makes it super easy to flip materials. **Hint**.

TEXT PARAMETERS

Text parameters are typically associated with **Labels**. A label is a symbol component you input from Revit's Annotations folder. This symbol, or Label, is then connected to a Text parameter, and this way you can change what the Label's Text shows. Additionally, the label can be connected to **Y/N** parameters for it to be visible or not. This part though is intended for use in the former, with Text parameters. So bring in a label into your family environment by:

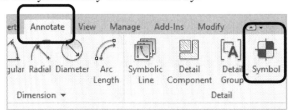

1. Press the Symbol button under the Annotate tab, and locate a Label family in Revit's imperial library. Once in, it should say Label, or '?' (question mark).
2. Touch the element (geometry)
3. Click on the square similarly as we did with other parameters, it looks like this:

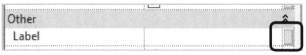

4. Select from a list of available Text parameters, press OK. Note that if not associated, you can write text here, and you would have a static label, not parametric, similar to how you can associate materials. (2) ways.

INTEGER PARAMETER

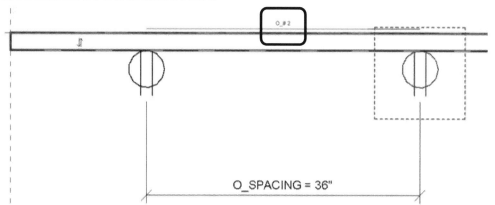

Integer parameters are often used with arrays. See image above. When you embed a family into your family, in this case, an outlet, it is possible to use a command called array. When you array an element, as shown above, you can associate the array number to an Integer parameter, and later in your project, you can change the number of outlets you want as you please. In this case, we have two. The steps are as follows:

1. Make your array.
2. Touch one of the elements (in this case an outlet).
3. You will see a number light-up/ appear (see above number 2).
4. Touch that, above a label field, will appear.
5. Touch the label drop-box, and a list of Integer parameters will display.

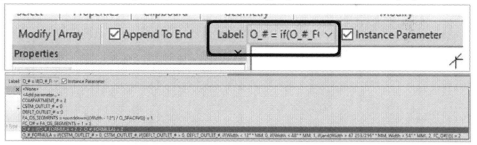

6. Select the one you want, and done.

From here on you can change the integer parameter's number, and the outlets will follow.

PART

3

THE BRAINS IN REVIT. AN OVERVIEW AND
EXAMPLES OF THE SYNTAX USED IN FORMULA
CREATION.

FORMULAS

RECAP

WHAT YOU NOW KNOW.

Let's do a recap of where you are now and move on from there. Using our trusty Movable table family shown here, let's imagine it's built with some basic parameters, WIDTH, DEPTH, and HEIGHT. Right now you know how to create and change these parameters effectively altering the MT's shape. You make duplicate types, and off you go, infinite MT sizes, so the question is:

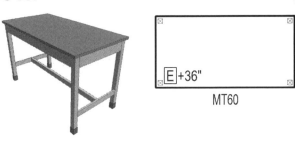

Why formulas? In one word, **CONTROL!**

Formulas give you infinite **control** as to what the end user can change, control to automate changes, to expand, or curtail capabilities, etc., etc. All this will become apparent as you move through the examples, for now, let's illustrate where you are; cause and effect, simple parameters with one outcome. Note many people never get past this step, so you are well on your way to knowing more than the average Revit user:

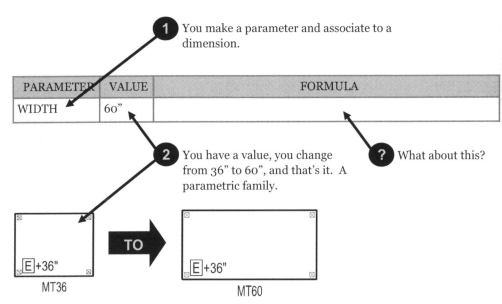

1. You make a parameter and associate to a dimension.

PARAMETER	VALUE	FORMULA
WIDTH	60"	

2. You have a value, you change from 36" to 60", and that's it. A parametric family.

? What about this?

WHAT YOU NOW KNOW (CONTINUED):

PARAMETER	VALUE	FORMULA
WIDTH	60"	

? What about this?

For now, the formula box is useless, the only thing you can use it for is to freeze a parameter. Go ahead and type in a number in the formula box, the result, it grays out the parameter. Whenever you make a formula the parameter will gray out. Why? Because that's what formulas do, they take control of a parameter and render it unchangeable by the human hand. The only thing that will change it is the formula, or in other words, other parameters in the formula field.

This graying out of a single parameter is a great tool as well, but let's circle back later, for now, let's keep moving forward and respond the original question:

What about this formula field? Let's analyze the **anatomy of a formula**. A formula at it's most basic and build on that.

ANATOMY OF A FORMULA

At its most basic, to create a formula you only need **two** parameters, a **trigger** parameter, and an **output** parameter:

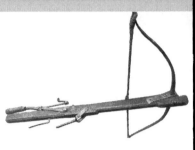

- The **trigger** parameter activates the formula (your manual input, you).
- The **output** parameter changes/ morphs the family.

The three most common parameters in formulas are Length parameters, Yes/ No parameters (visibility), and Text parameters. The '**output**' parameter is the parameter associated with the actual family, e.g., dimensions, geometry visibility, and labels. **Output** parameters are typically grayed out by the formula controlling them.

The **trigger** parameter is never grayed out since it controls the formula that controls the **output** parameter. Don't get confused there's still only (2) parameters. Let's illustrate:

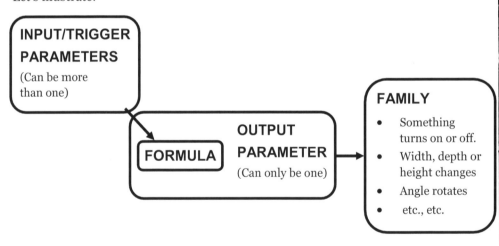

If this is not clear don't worry, you are at the beginning, and all this will sink in organically as you move through examples. You can always circle back once you review some examples.

INTENTIONAL BREAK

SIMPLE FORMULAS

95% of the time, even on complicated formulas you will learn later, you will be using very simple math like:

A. Summing (+)
B. Subtracting (-)
C. Multiplying (*)
D. Dividing (/)
E. Equal to (=)
F. Greater than (>)
G. Less than (<)

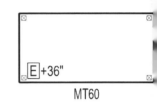
MT60

Now, there is the ability to use Pi, square root, logarithms, etc., etc., but for most mortals, this basic syntax will suffice.

EXAMPLE 01 - A BASIC FORMULA - PERFECT RECTANGLE

Let's say you have a family (the MT in this case) and you want to **control** its shape so that it's always a perfect rectangle. You have two options:

1. You can rely on the end user to never forget to change the DEPTH to half of the WIDTH, always (human error).
2. You make a formula to automate the DEPTH to always be half of the WIDTH (no human error).

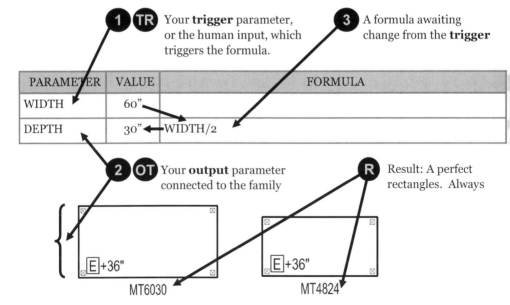

EXAMPLES 02 - A BASIC FORMULA - VARIATIONS

1. A SLIGHTLY DEEPER TABLE
Using the summing (+) function, you get a table that is always 12" deeper than it's WIDTH.

PARAMETER	VALUE	FORMULA
WIDTH	60"	
DEPTH	72"	WIDTH+12"

2. A SLIGHTLY SLENDER TABLE
Using the subtracting (-) function, you get a table that is always 12" less deep than it's WIDTH

PARAMETER	VALUE	FORMULA
WIDTH	60"	
DEPTH	48"	WIDTH - 12"

3. A PERFECT SQUARE
Merely writing the parameter in the formula box, you're guaranteed a perfect square (=). The equal sign is implied.

PARAMETER	VALUE	FORMULA
WIDTH	60"	
DEPTH	60"	WIDTH

4. TWICE AS DEEP
Using the multiplying (*) function you get a table that is always twice as deep as it's WIDTH

PARAMETER	VALUE	FORMULA
WIDTH	60"	
DEPTH	120"	WIDTH*2

EXAMPLE 03 - MIXING PARAMETERS - AUTOMATIC SUPPORT

Let's say we want a pair of posts on our movable table to hold the middle as WIDTH expands past a certain WIDTH. Additionally, you want to **control** precisely when this happens, at or above 8'-0". You have two options:

1. You can rely on the end user to never forget to click on a Y/N parameter (POSTS) every time the family reaches 8'-0", and never forget (human error).
2. You write a formula to automate the parameter POST to turn on automatically when your criteria are met (no human error).

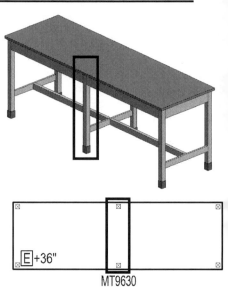

You will need (2) parameters, a **Length** parameter and a **Y/N** parameter.

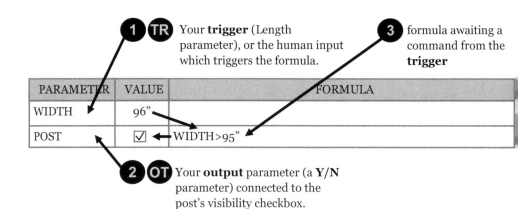

1 TR Your **trigger** (Length parameter), or the human input which triggers the formula.

3 formula awaiting a command from the **trigger**

PARAMETER	VALUE	FORMULA
WIDTH	96"	
POST	☑	WIDTH>95"

2 OT Your **output** parameter (a Y/N parameter) connected to the post's visibility checkbox.

NOTE:
The WIDTH is set to **trigger** when WIDTH is longer than 95". Why did I set it 1" below the 96" (8'-0") mark? This is because I want the post to turn on at or above 96" WIDTH. Had I set the formula to 'WIDTH=96'" then the post would have lit up **ONLY** at 96" and then turned off after that.

EXAMPLES 04 - MIXING PARAMETERS - CYCLING

Cycling is a method whereby merely using (1) **integer** parameter as your **trigger**, you can cycle through infinite visibility (Y/N) parameters. Let's illustrate:

You'll need an integer parameter and as many Y/N parameters as you want to **trigger**/ cycle through.

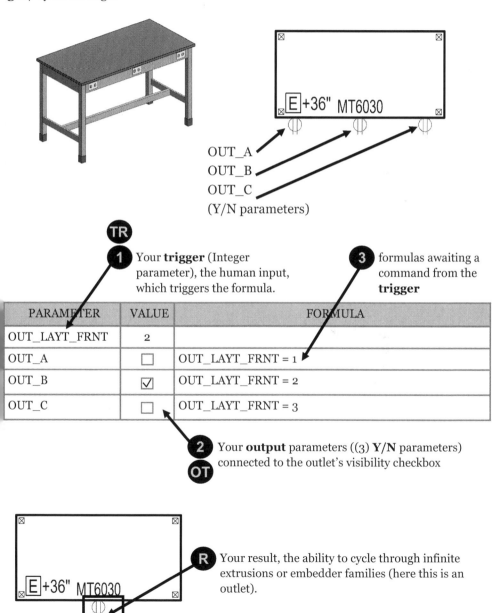

OUT_A
OUT_B
OUT_C
(Y/N parameters)

1 Your **trigger** (Integer parameter), the human input, which triggers the formula.

3 formulas awaiting a command from the **trigger**

PARAMETER	VALUE	FORMULA
OUT_LAYT_FRNT	2	
OUT_A	☐	OUT_LAYT_FRNT = 1
OUT_B	☑	OUT_LAYT_FRNT = 2
OUT_C	☐	OUT_LAYT_FRNT = 3

2 Your **output** parameters ((3) **Y/N** parameters) connected to the outlet's visibility checkbox

R Your result, the ability to cycle through infinite extrusions or embedder families (here this is an outlet).

COMPLEX FORMULAS

Complex formulas involve functions and conditional statements. NOW... just because I named this section COMPLEX FORMULAS, this does not mean that they are **hard** formulas. They are actually very, very, easy once you learn to use the functions and conditional statements as we did in the previous section. In reality, the formulas just **look difficult**. You will quickly discover **they are not**.

FUNCTIONS AND CONDITIONAL STATEMENTS

I always thought of the following syntax as a little box or **container** that houses your formulas/ parameters and outside there is a guy who tells the contents of the box how to behave. Let's quickly list all these functions, and then I'll explain which ones you will use 95% of the time, and which ones here and there.

A. If (A,B,C)
B. Not (A)
C. And (A,B)
D. Or (A,B)
E. Round (#)
F. RoundUp (#)
G. RoundDown (#)

IMPORTANCE BY RANK

❶ IF(A,B,C) - USED 60%

By far the most important function in Revit formulas. This is **THE** king of functionality. You will use this function to **boss** around all other functions. This is a conditional statement, which basically lets you turn math or code into how you think, e.g., If (I press this button, then turn OFF, if not, then ON). Simple, it will make sense later, just know it is important.

❷ NOT(A) - AND(A,B) - OR(A,B) - USED 35%.

Although these functions are used independently, you 'll find that most of the time they act as **support** for the aforementioned **king**, If (A,B,C).

❸ ROUND FUNCTIONS - USED 5%.

These last (3) functions round numbers with decimals up or down. I've found these three are sparingly used, though I can see their importance for some tasks.

INTENTIONAL BREAK

FUNCTION EXAMPLES

Let's begin our examples from least important (Round ( ) functions) to most important (IF ( ) function), this way we can get the easy stuff out of the way, and we can focus/ concentrate on the more complex, exciting, and functional aspects of formulas once we reviewed the easy material.

EXAMPLE 01 - ROUND FUNCTIONS

Round functions (3) let you round numbers. This function enables you to turn any number from a decimal number like 36.7 to a whole number 37. Easy enough, but before you begin, there are caveats. These **do not work with dimensions!** And others; the round function only works with the following parameters:

A. Number
B. Currency
C. Slope

That said..., there are ways around these caveats. You can multiply by 1, or divide by 1 to solve this issue, but for now, let's get back to functions, and we'll circle back to neutralizing the horribly pesky 'inconsistent units' error under part 5, common errors section. Don't get discouraged, there is usually always a way around these errors. On to examples.

 ROUND (#)

The round function rounds a parameter up and down. From, say, 1.1 to 1.4 it will round down to 1, and from 1.5 to 1.9 it will round up to 2. See below example.

Note:
1. We are using a number parameter to both **trigger** and **output** the formula.
2. Either parameter can be named entirely different. It could have easily been, parameter A & B. The critical thing is to know who triggers the formula and who changes/ morphs the family.

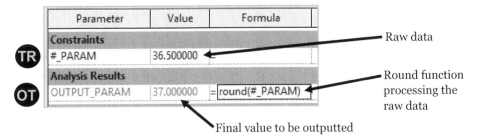

B **ROUNDDOWN (#)**

The rounddown function rounds a parameter down. From, 1.1 to 1.9 it will always round down to 1. See below example.

Parameter	Value	Formula
Constraints		
TR #_PARAM	36.500000	=
Analysis Results		
OT OUTPUT_PARAM	36.000000	=rounddown(#_PARAM)

C **ROUNDUP (#)**

The rounddown function rounds a parameter down. From, 1.1 to 1.9 it will always round up to 2. See below example.

Parameter	Value	Formula
Constraints		
TR #_PARAM	36.500000	=
Analysis Results		
OT OUTPUT_PARAM	37.000000	= roundup(#_PARAM)

EXAMPLE 02 - NOT(A) FUNCTION

Very, very simple, and highly useful function. When you create (2) Y/N parameters, you can set one to always do the opposite of the other parameter. Basically, you get a seesaw effect.

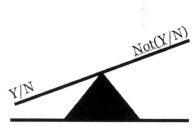

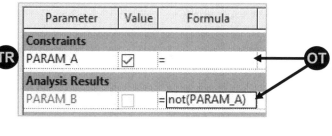

In theory, both of these can be output parameters connected merely to (2) distinct geometry. **Hint**.

EXAMPLE 03 - OR(A,B,C, ETC., ETC.)

The or(A,B) function lets you activate a parameter when, well an infinite amount of things happen. Could be if either one of two or more Y/N parameter were to turn on, or if either one of two, or more LENGTH parameters were to say be >36" or <60". In this case, the **output** parameter would not activate between 36" and 60"... anywho, on to graphical examples, words are no fun.

Lets circle back to the simple parameters example on cycling. In that example, we learn to cycle through Y/N parameters using an INTEGER parameter. Let's go back to that example and expand its capabilities with the 'or' function.

Here is what I want to do. I want to use an INTEGER parameter so when I press 1, one outlet turns on, 2, two outlets turn on, 3, three outlets turn on, 4, one outlet turns on (a different one this time), and 5, one outlet turns on (different one again). Let's diagram this on the table, I would typically do this on paper.

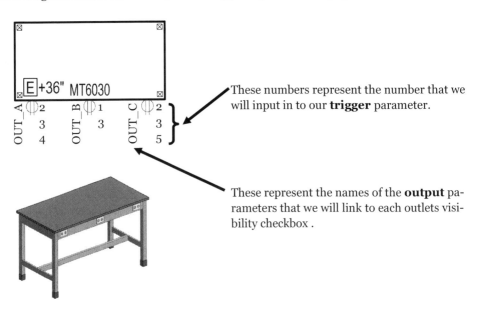

These numbers represent the number that we will input in to our **trigger** parameter.

These represent the names of the **output** parameters that we will link to each outlets visibility checkbox.

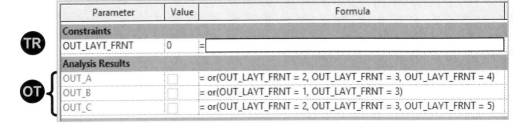

R RESULTS

Parameter	Value	Formula
Constraints		
OUT_LAYT_FRNT	1	=
Analysis Results		
OUT_A	☐	= or(OUT_LAYT_FRNT = 2, OUT_LAYT_FRNT = 3, OUT_LAYT_FRNT = 4)
OUT_B	☑	= or(OUT_LAYT_FRNT = 1, OUT_LAYT_FRNT = 3)
OUT_C	☐	= or(OUT_LAYT_FRNT = 2, OUT_LAYT_FRNT = 3, OUT_LAYT_FRNT = 5)

E +36" MT6030

Parameter	Value	Formula
Constraints		
OUT_LAYT_FRNT	2	=
Analysis Results		
OUT_A	☑	= or(OUT_LAYT_FRNT = 2, OUT_LAYT_FRNT = 3, OUT_LAYT_FRNT = 4)
OUT_B	☐	= or(OUT_LAYT_FRNT = 1, OUT_LAYT_FRNT = 3)
OUT_C	☑	= or(OUT_LAYT_FRNT = 2, OUT_LAYT_FRNT = 3, OUT_LAYT_FRNT = 5)

E +36" MT6030

Parameter	Value	Formula
Constraints		
OUT_LAYT_FRNT	3	=
Analysis Results		
OUT_A	☑	= or(OUT_LAYT_FRNT = 2, OUT_LAYT_FRNT = 3, OUT_LAYT_FRNT = 4)
OUT_B	☑	= or(OUT_LAYT_FRNT = 1, OUT_LAYT_FRNT = 3)
OUT_C	☑	= or(OUT_LAYT_FRNT = 2, OUT_LAYT_FRNT = 3, OUT_LAYT_FRNT = 5)

E +36" MT6030

Parameter	Value	Formula
Constraints		
OUT_LAYT_FRNT	4	=
Analysis Results		
OUT_A	☑	= or(OUT_LAYT_FRNT = 2, OUT_LAYT_FRNT = 3, OUT_LAYT_FRNT = 4)
OUT_B	☐	= or(OUT_LAYT_FRNT = 1, OUT_LAYT_FRNT = 3)
OUT_C	☐	= or(OUT_LAYT_FRNT = 2, OUT_LAYT_FRNT = 3, OUT_LAYT_FRNT = 5)

E +36" MT6030

Parameter	Value	Formula
Constraints		
OUT_LAYT_FRNT	5	=
Analysis Results		
OUT_A	☐	= or(OUT_LAYT_FRNT = 2, OUT_LAYT_FRNT = 3, OUT_LAYT_FRNT = 4)
OUT_B	☐	= or(OUT_LAYT_FRNT = 1, OUT_LAYT_FRNT = 3)
OUT_C	☑	= or(OUT_LAYT_FRNT = 2, OUT_LAYT_FRNT = 3, OUT_LAYT_FRNT = 5)

E +36" MT6030

NOTE:

The **trigger** name: OUT_LAYT_FRNT, which stands for outlet layout front. This formula is used for LEFT, RIGHT, and BACK, for a total of (4) **triggers**, and (12) **output** parameters, e.g. OUT_LAYT_LEFT, or RIGHT. Ultimately the **output** parameter numbers don't really matter, only the **trigger**. The end user will just be looking for the **triggers**. This cycling methods, in essence, lets you collapse (12) Y/N parameters into (4) INTEGER parameters, **fun**.

EXAMPLE 04 - AND(A,B,C, ETC., ETC.)

This is another straightforward function. It will activate a parameter when two commands are met, e.g., Let's say you have our trusty MT below. When at 36" high, the apron is 4", but when dropped to 30" it will need a 2" apron to avoid knee knocking. A simple formula can change the apron height from 4" to 2" at 30" high, now, the monkey wrench. We need to add a little scallop for when this happens, and we have electrical outlets. A simple And() formula can fix this.

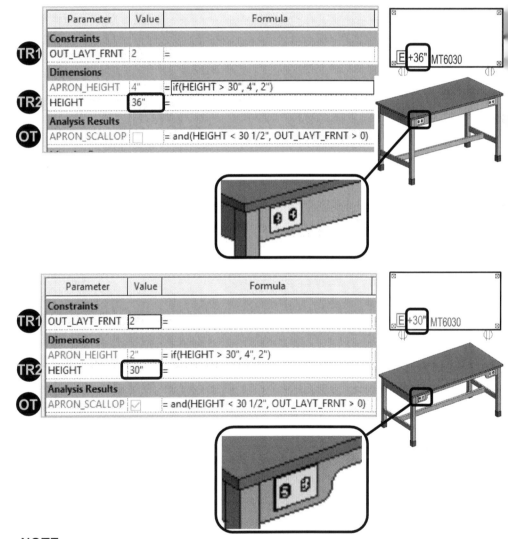

NOTE:

The APRON_SCALLOP **output** parameter needs (2) things to happen to activate. 1. HEIGHT parameter (Length) to be smaller than 30.5" and 2. an outlet to be on, which occurs when the integer parameter OUT_LAYT_FRNT is higher than 0 as shown on the previous example.

EXAMPLE 05 - IF(A,B,C, ETC., ETC.)

The If ( ) function is by far **THE KING** of all functions. As stated before, 'by far, the most important function in Revit formulas'. This is **THE** king of functionality. You will use this function to **boss** around all other functions.' In a way, the If ( ) function helps you truly turn a written plan in **simple English**, into functional code for Revit to understand. I know, you don't see it yet, but **patience**, we will explore this a lot. You will see how all the previous functions work together under this function, to do some pretty interesting things. Let's see how this function is put together, and let's see what we can do with it.

A) THE ANATOMY OF THE IF ( ) FUNCTION

	PARAMETER	VALUE	FORMULA
TR	WIDTH	60"	
OT	DEPTH	30"	IF (WIDTH>72" , 36" , 30")

If WIDTH is greater than 72"

Then (comma)

DEPTH will be 36"

If not! (comma)

DEPTH will be 30"

E +36"

MT60

R) Width is 60"; smaller than 72", so the default 30" remains.

In my mind, I always think of the commas as words, (as shown above) that help transition the conditional statement from one to another (**Hint**). Note the circled last (3rd) part of the if ( ) function. This last piece is **unique** because this value closes the conditional statement. This is the default Length; the **resting** Length. This value awaits for a formula to overpower it, but until that happens, this is the default value for the DEPTH parameter.

As we get into examples you will learn that many, many things come between if, and the **'closer'** value, and as everything that comes before the **'closer'** can change, and be insanely long, one thing is always constant; you always needs a resting/ default **'closing'** value at the end to rest your parameter on.

B. EMBEDDING CONDITIONAL STATEMENTS

Similarly to the And ( ), and Or ( ) functions, you can embed not only other If( ) functions, but **ALL** previously discussed functions infinitely, making this one **THE most powerful** function in Revit. Below is an example of the If( ) function with an embedded If ( ) function.

Note once my formulas develop a certain complexity, I will write in plain English what I want to achieve and then set out to make it happen. This is a great way to plan for your formulas, for example:

In English: I want a table that its default DEPTH is 24", but:
- When the WIDTH is equal or greater than 36", the DEPTH will be 30".
- When the WIDTH is equal or greater than 60", the DEPTH will be 36".

In essence at certain widths, the table will be a predefined depth. Think of it as if a manufacturer only sold tables in specific depths and widths. Below is the outcome.

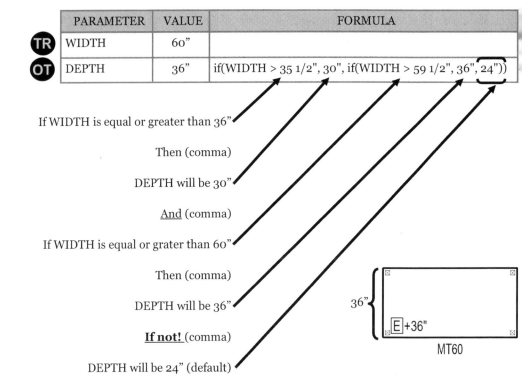

A COUPLE OF THINGS TO NOTE:

PARAMETER	VALUE	FORMULA
TR WIDTH	60"	
OT DEPTH	36"	if(WIDTH > 35 1/2", 30", if(WIDTH > 59 1/2", 36", **24"**))

1. The **trigger** widths are 0.5" below where I want them to **trigger**. Why? This is because I want the formula to trigger **AT** 36" and at 60", otherwise it would **trigger** above these dimensions, not equal or greater than. **Hint**.

2. Both if ( ) statements contradict each other. The formula ushers a change above 36" in WIDTH. This should be the end of the discussion, right? No. It works because **formulas are read from left to right**. So whatever is on the left is more **powerful**, than whatever is on the right. When 36" in WIDTH hits, it skips the 60" command, but when above 60" in WIDTH hits, then the power is given back to the command to the left. **Think about it. This is really important to understand.** This did not matter before the if ( ) function.

3. Look at the number of parenthesis to the far right (2). As you add if ( ) functions inside the parenthesis, you will notice that for every if ( ) function you embed, you need to add a closing parenthesis at the end. In the example above there are (2) closing parenthesis for the (2) if( ) statements.

PARAMETER	VALUE	FORMULA
WIDTH	60"	
DEPTH	36"	**if(**WIDTH > 35 1/2", 30", **if(**WIDTH > 59 1/2", 36", 24"))

As mentioned before, many, many things come between if( ) and the **'closer'** value, and as everything that comes before the **'closer'** can change, and be insanely long one thing is always constant; you always need a resting/ default **'closing'** value at the end to rest your parameter on.

PART 4

A SET OF TRIED AND TESTED FORMULAS AND
FORMULA COMBINATIONS THAT CAN BE TAILORED
TO OODLES OF FAMILY SCENARIOS.

FORMULA IDEAS

ANATOMY OF A FORMULA PART DEUX

Similar to the first installment of 'Anatomy of a formula' at the beginning of the **formulas part**; this second installment has been added as a guide to illustrate how formulas grow in complexity. Again **don't fear complexity**, complexity does not mean hard. This section will introduce the concept of **support** parameters which help open up formulas to greater **functionality**.

The next three diagrams aim to illustrate principles you will see throughout the **Formula ideas** part. If it doesn't make sense yet don't obsess, look through the 'support and graying' out section and then come back. These will make more sense. The intent is to start showing these relationships up front.

A) ORIGINAL FORMULA ANATOMY

Below is the original Anatomy of a formula. It illustrates how the **input** parameters (which can be more than one) act as the catalyst and **triggers** the formula within the **output** parameter. The **output** parameter is what ultimately changes the family.

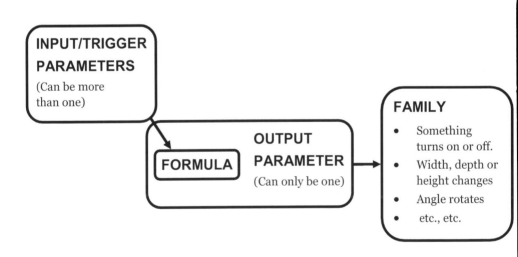

B) FORMULA WITH SUPPORT PARAMETERS

In this diagram, we see the same layout as 'A,' except we have support parameters that feed the **output** formula as well. The **support** parameters in this diagram are simple, in that they are static, grayed out parameters, like a Y/N or a number that is not really smart or dynamic, just something simple we need to abbreviate in the **OT** formula.

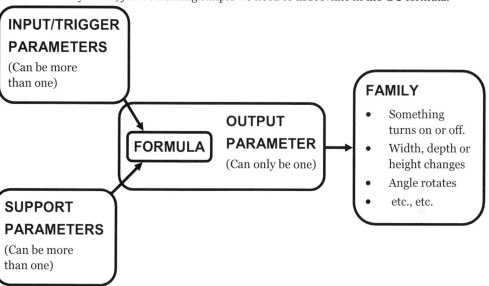

C) FORMULA WITH SMART SUPPORT PARAMETERS

In this diagram we see the same layout as 'B,' except the support parameters have formulas that are influenced by the input parameters, and then affects the **OT** parameter's formula.

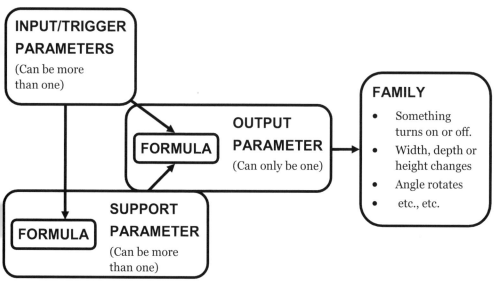

PROXY PARAMETERS

Proxy is the authority to represent someone else or a figure that can be used to represent the value of something else in a calculation. In essence, someone acting as someone else. This is precisely what we will do now but with parameters and formulas.

As we saw in previous examples, when you apply a formula, it grays out a parameter. So far we have been using the WIDTH parameter to modify the DEPTH parameter for many examples, but what if we wanted to use the WIDTH parameter to alter the WIDTH parameter. What? The answer is, you can't. You would get an error. The solution is a proxy parameter. One parameter telling another parameter clone what to do.

Here is the problem we will be solving with our proxy parameter using our trusty movable table. We need:

1. All movable tables to be 36" high (standing height).
2. Some movable tables to be 30" high (sitting height).
3. Per code, 5% have to be 34" high (ADA accessible).

So, the manufacturer ONLY makes these (3) heights. Now, I want to curtail the end users from making a 27" or 40" high table. I want to **control** the end user's ability to break my family. One solution is to make the (3 height) types beforehand and gray them out. But what if I want a typeless component and the end user to just type-in the HEIGHT as he goes along? In other applications, I have used this method to eliminate (30+) types, and render a virtual typeless component. We will explore that later, for now, we will use this example to make a (3) height errorless component. Don't worry, it will make sense shortly, here is the formula:

Parameter	Value	Formula
Dimensions		
HEIGHT_USE	27"	=
HEIGHT	30"	= if(HEIGHT_USE > 34 1/2", 36", if(HEIGHT_USE > 30", 34", 30"))

THE BREAKDOWN

Parameter	Value	Formula
Dimensions		
HEIGHT_USE	27"	=
HEIGHT	30"	= if(HEIGHT_USE > 34 1/2", 36", if(HEIGHT_USE > 30", 34", 30"))

Remember formulas are read from left to right, so in this formula the **trigger** is set to 27", therefore everything to the left does not meet the formula's criteria, so it defaults to 30", as the parameters of the formula are met, the functions to the right will begin to activate in order.

The rules where design such that if above 30", 34", and if above 34", 36"if **not!** Then drop to 30". Simple but powerful.

Now you can schedule your components by HEIGHT and get an accurate reading, even if the user erroneously were to type in 27" or 40", you would never get an unmanufacturable table.

Another plus is if both parameters are set to **instance,** you do not need to make types. Just type-in the Height you need, and you are done.

Below is another example that yields the same result. I include this example to show how you can get to the same result with a different thought process. We all don't think alike. Formulas are a result of how you think. As you grow in experience, you'll become much better at making tight and concise formulas.

Naming the parameters is entirely up to what makes sense to you. For example, I thought of naming the HEIGHT_USE as HEIGHT_CSTM or HEIGHT. (note period in the end), that is entirely up to you.

ALTERNATE FORMULA SAME RESULT
In this scenario the resting HEIGHT is 36", and you sort of build to it from left to right. The above example I like because it teaches you that the strength of the conditional statement is from left to right. **Very important to know.**

Parameter	Value	Formula
Dimensions		
HEIGHT_USE	27"	=
HEIGHT	30"	= if(HEIGHT_USE < 30 1/2", 30", if(HEIGHT_USE < 36", 34", 36"))

INSTANCE AND TYPE PARAMETER TRICK

Piggybacking off our previous example where we **controlled** the end user's ability to change a components HEIGHT. In this example, I will teach you how to overwrite the HEIGHT formula we wrote in the previous section with a second **instance** parameter. THEN, overwrite both of those parameters with a third **type** parameter. I know, I know, **WHAT?** Basically having a HEIGHT parameter that you can overwrite per instance or per type. The best of both worlds. Let's illustrate.

1. Using the proxy parameter example, we have a component that can only have (3) heights, 30", 34", and 36".

2. Now I will make a second parameter named HEIGHT_INST which when higher than 0" it will overwrite (overpower) the previous formula only once, for that one instance.

3. Then I will make a third parameter named HEIGHT_TYPE that when higher than 0" it will overwrite (overpower) both the original formula and HEIGHT_INST. When HEIGHT_TYPE is greater than 0", then HEIGHT_TYPE will trump all other parameters. You need to make duplicates for HEIGHT_TYPE otherwise, it will overwrite **ALL** formula and instance parameters. Don't worry, if you 0" HEIGHT_TYPE again, all the other parameters return. Don't get it. Don't worry, just do it, flex it, and it will make sense.

I use this method all the time. Most of my families don't even use types anymore, only when I want to highlight a particular type, and still, I have a wide range of capabilities. The important thing is to be able to schedule your components by HEIGHT, WIDTH, DEPTH, on CASTERS, with DRAWERS, etc.

See below formula for this scenario. Yes, you can start to see that these can get long, on the next page we will break down all this more legibly.

Parameter	Value	Formula
Dimensions		
HEIGHT_INST (default)	0"	=
HEIGHT_TYPE	0"	=
HEIGHT_USE (default)	27"	=
HEIGHT (default)	30"	= if(HEIGHT_TYPE > 0", HEIGHT_TYPE, if(HEIGHT_INST > 0", HEIGHT_INST, if(HEIGHT_USE > 34 1/2", 36", if(HEIGHT_USE > 30", 34", 30"))))

THE BREAKDOWN

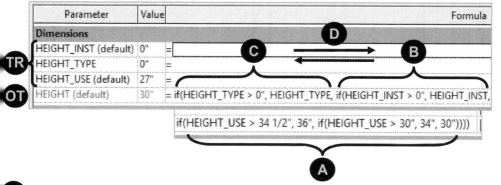

A PARAMETER FROM PROXY PARAMETERS SECTION - INSTANCE
This whole section is nothing more than the original proxy parameter we wrote in the previous section

B INSTANCE PARAMETER
This section will overwrite (overpower) the (A) section when HEIGHT_INST is greater than 0".

C TYPE PARAMETER
This section will overwrite (overpower) the (A) & (B) sections when HEIGHT_TYPE is greater than 0".

NOTE! (C) Is the only **type** parameter, which means that it will overwrite (overpower) all the components throughout the project, not just one. The cool thing about this formula is that all changes revert back merely by typing 0" again.

D REVERSE PARAMETER HIERARCHY
If you reverse (C) & (B), the instance parameter will overpower the type parameter, try it. **Hint.**

SEE BELOW FORMULAS OVERPOWERING PREDEFINED HEIGHTS.

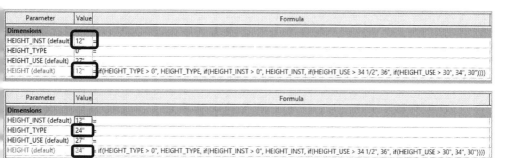

MAKE ANYTHING METRIC

This is a very simple formula that as the title states, will make anything metric, and of course by anything I mean any length from imperial to metric and back.

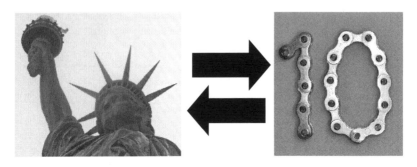

Imperial   Metric

FORMULA

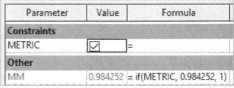

Not activated   Activated
(default)

All family templates I build have this formula baked-in as a default. When you make the **trigger** parameter named METRIC (a Y/N parameter) a **shared parameter,** you can create a schedule in your project that with a flick of a button, or buttons, will turn all your families metric. All the families that employ this formula will automatically "**shrink to metric.**"

Let's look at where the 0.984252 number comes from, the concept behind "**shrinking to metric,**" and finally how to use it. The METRIC parameter is something the end user would know about and see. The MM number parameter is a **support** parameter that you can employ again and again once it is set up. If you just want to know how to use the formula jump right in, otherwise read through the concept behind it so you can learn what it's doing. Note, the next section goes into more detail as to what **support** parameters are and do, for now, let's just focus on MM (number parameter).

SHRINKING TO METRIC AND 0.984252

The concept of "**shrinking to metric**" is actually straightforward. Let's say you have a 60" wide table, and you want a Y/N parameter that when turned on, will shrink your table to 30" wide. A simple way to achieve this would be to multiply the WIDTH by 0.5. In fact, by multiplying by 0.5, you ensure that no matter what the WIDTH is, the WIDTH will always be half the WIDTH when the Y/N parameter is activated. This is the same concept we used to "**shrink to metric.**" Let's illustrate.

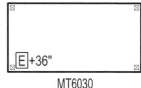
MT6030

IMPERIAL	MILLIMETERS
12"	304.8mm
60"	1524mm

See table above. 12" or 1'-0" is exactly 304.8mm, and 60" or 5'-0" is exactly 1524mm. If the table above (MT6030) were to be built in Europe, they would not manufacture a table at **1524mm** wide. They would manufacture a table at **1500mm** wide. So the conversion from imperial to metric for building-purposes is 12" or 1'-0" = 300mm. The table and your cheat sheet would look like this:

IMPERIAL	MILLIMETERS (BUILDABLE)
12"	300mm
60"	1500mm

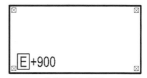
MT1500x750

Now you see, we need the 1524mm table to "**shrink to metric**" by 24mm. Armed with this knowledge and the concept of multiplying by 0.5 explained above. We need to find a number that when multiplied by whatever number will " **shrink to metric.**" This number is... you guess it **0.984252.**

IMPERIAL	MILLIMETERS (BUILDABLE)
.9842519685"	25MM

The 0.984252 is actually 25MM in inches. Since 1" = 25.4mm, then 0.984252" = 25mm, or the rounded off version of the imperial number you are trying to convert. Revit will not accept the full number noted above, though what it does recognize is enough for the conversion. A lot of fuzz to get here but powerful stuff. The question is; so how do you use it? Let's illustrate.

HOW TO USE MM

Let's use the formula from the 'proxy parameters' section and make it metric ready:

PROXY PARAMETER FORMULA

Parameter	Value	Formula
Dimensions		
HEIGHT_USE	27"	=
HEIGHT	30"	= if(HEIGHT_USE > 34 1/2", 36", if(HEIGHT_USE > 30", 34", 30"))

EXAMPLE 01

Depending on your formula you can multiply at the end by **MM**. When at rest it multiplies by 1 and when active by 0.984252. Note that the whole first part of the formula is **contained** within a parenthesis then multiplied by MM. I find that encasing formulas between parenthesis and then multiplying or dividing, keeps things cleaner. **Hint**.

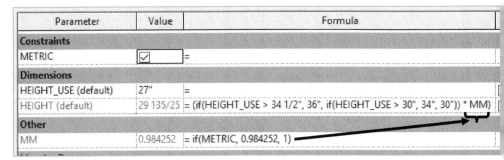

EXAMPLE 02

Placing **MM** within the formula wherever you intend the change to take place.

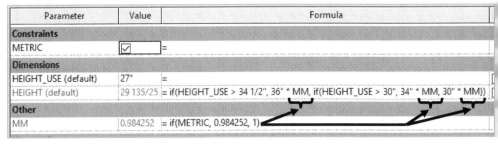

These are just (2) examples. The formula is simple and powerful and can be used widely throughout. I recommend making it part of your template, so you have **MM** lock, loaded and ready to use.

INTENTIONAL BREAK

SUPPORT AND GRAYING OUT PARAMETERS

SUPPORT PARAMETERS

Support parameters are parameters that you build to help the **output** parameter get the job done. Let's just say that the **output** parameter is **Elvis**, and the support parameters are the **roadies**. They are not meant to be seen, but the show would not go on without them.

Parameter	Value	Formula
Constraints		
METRIC	☐	=
Other		
MM	1.000000	= if(METRIC, 0.984252, 1)
OFF	☐	= 0 + 0 = 1
ON	☑	= 0 + 0 = 0

See image above. Here are (3) examples of simple support parameters. As seen in the previous section 'make anything metric,' I typically have these support parameters lock and loaded in all my family templates, just because they are so universal. The ON and OFF parameters helps when writing formulas because it allows you to just write the syntax in English for turning a Y/N parameter ON and OFF. For example, in the 'Simple parameters' section, we had a table that when wider than 96" center support legs would turn on. The formula was:

PARAMETER	VALUE	FORMULA
WIDTH	96"	
POST	☑	WIDTH>95"

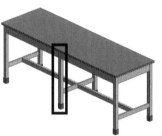

ALTERNATE PHRASING WITH SUPPORT PARAMETERS.

PARAMETER	VALUE	FORMULA
WIDTH	96"	
POST	☑	IF(WIDTH>95", ON, OFF)

Now, in the first example, the IF ( ) statement is implied, and truth be told it is more elegant than the second example, but in the second example, it just seems like regular English. By merely having (2) Y/N parameters in your template that allow you to just write ON to turn something on or OFF to turn something off, it really makes a big difference when writing formulas.

Now, these (3) parameters I have in my family templates by default but in no way are these the only ones. Depending on the task at hand, I keep adding support parameters as the components complexity demands it. They just sit and accumulate at the bottom ignored by the end user, and eventually by me.

GRAYING OUT PARAMETERS

Why? Why is graying out parameters important? The answer; user error. In the image to the right we grayed out ON and OFF on purpose, the MM is grayed out because of the **trigger** parameter. In theory, you could have a slew of support parameters just sitting there not grayed out but beware, not graying parameters out means leaving them exposed to user changes. If someone were to turn the 'ON' parameter off, for example, this could fundamentally alter ALL the parameters where you used 'ON.' **Catastrophic**! Graying them out **protects** you from this exposure.

Parameter	Value	Formula
Constraints		
METRIC	☐	=
Other		
MM	1.000000	= if(METRIC, 0.984252, 1)
OFF	☐	= 0 + 0 = 1
ON	☑	= 0 + 0 = 0

Sometimes you may be tempted to not gray out **support parameters** thinking, "it would be cool to be able to alter them on the fly in the future." Don't. This will bite you in the butt. Better yet **gray them out** and just open the family when you need to adjust. Simple and safe.

EXAMPLE OF GRAYING DIFFERENT TYPES OF PARAMETERS

A. For the Y/N parameters, you merely add a mathematical equation. If true, it grays out 'ON.' If false, it grays out 'OFF.'

B. For the text parameter, which we'll go into detail later, you just add (2) quote signs " " for a **blank** result and if you want to gray out a word, just add the word in between the (2) quotation marks, e.g., "word here" or as shown below.

C. For all other number base parameters merely adding a number will suffice.

Parameter	Value	Formula
Text		
TEXT	THIS IS BLANK NOW	= "THIS IS BLANK NOW"
TEXT_BLANK		= ""
Dimensions		
LENGTH	36"	= 36"
Other		
NUMBER	36.000000	= 36
OFF	☐	= 0 + 0 = 1
ON	☑	= 0 + 0 = 0

HORIZONTAL OR VERTICAL FORMUALS?

As you continue making complex formulas, you will soon realize that they can get very, very lengthy. Now that is not necessarily a bad thing, you just need to make a decision with some of your formulas if you are:

A. Building horizontally or
B. Building vertically

Quick disclaimer, I am a fan of long horizontal formulas, though you really do need one of those new wide monitors to read them. When that becomes an issue is when I begin to break them up vertically. In the previous section '**support and graying out parameters**' you can already see an example of vertically organized formulas where instead of embedding 0+0=0 in the formula to turn on a Y/N parameter, you are summoning another parameter below to get a more slender formula on your **output** parameter.

See next page example for an alteration to the formula we used in the previous section. At a simple glance, we can see that it is already becoming lengthy. Nothing wrong with that. Lengthy formulas are actually easier to read sometimes. That said, unless you have one of those really wide monitors previously mentioned, this can actually start to become cumbersome. The solution is **support parameters** and verticalization.

A HORIZONTAL

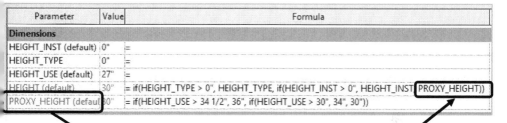

Break off point

B VERTICAL

A simple example, though the idea is to get you thinking where can I cut, and break down? Now I named the parameter PROXY_HEIGHT though it could easily have been the letter A, or PH, or anything else to further shorten the formula. As long as you know what the abbreviation means that's all that matters. I do prefer a more descriptive name though.

See below two examples with the aforementioned ON/OFF **support** parameters from the previous section.

A HORIZONTAL

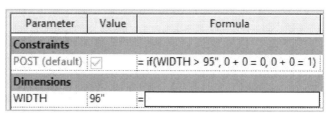

B VERTICAL

NEXT LEVEL FORMULA
WIDTH WITH INTERVALS

This section will integrate most of the concepts we have visited before. This formula (or group of formulas) is long vertically and horizontally. It involves different types of parameters and gosh darn it, it likes itself (SNL reference). But seriously, it is work. Now don't stress, you got this. If you can follow, I think we're done.

When I get an idea, I always write it down in plain English to plan exactly what I want to accomplish. This is really important, especially if you know it is complicated. Let's list what we want to achieve and remember, as long as the formulas work no matter how many acrobatics you need to do to get there, **the formula only needs to work once**. And all those support parameters you end up making are usually just for **one output**. It's all about that **output parameter**. So, on to the task at hand.

I want a movable table that:

A. Widens on precise intervals, e.g., every 6", since the manufacturer only manufactures the table in 6" increments.
B. At it's minimum the WIDTH will be 36" and at it's maximum 96" wide.
C. I can overwrite it via instance and type parameters (as we showed before).
D. And, I can make it metric with a click of a button (as we showed before).

Not too much to ask for right? Below is the formula (s), before the breakdown.

Parameter	Value	Formula
Constraints		
METRIC	☑	=
Dimensions		
WIDTH_TYPE	0"	=
WIDTH_INST (default)	0"	=
WIDTH_USER (default)	36"	=
Analysis Results		
WIDTH (default)	36"	= if(WIDTH_INST > 0", WIDTH_INST, if(WIDTH_TYPE > 0", WIDTH_TYPE, WI_INTERVALS * MM))
Other		
MM	1.000000	= 1
WIDTH_HIGH	96"	= 96"
WIDTH_LOW	36"	= 36"
WI_RATE	6"	= 6"
WI_INTERVALS (default)	36"	= if(WI_ROUNDED# < WIDTH_LOW, WIDTH_LOW, if(WI_ROUNDED# > WIDTH_HIGH, WIDTH_HIGH, WI_ROUNDED#))
WI_INTEGER (default)	6	= WIDTH_USER * 1 / WI_RATE
WI_ROUNDED# (default)	36"	= WI_RATE * WI_INTEGER

THE BREAKDOWN

First thing first, see below. For all the hard work that will go in producing a formula like this, the only thing that the end user will ever care about (think back to the **IOS** analogy) is the **trigger** formulas. That is great, that is what we want, that is why we grayed out **everything**. When you see it this way, it looks pretty simple. Also, note the X'd-out/ grayed out portion. These are all support parameters except for the **output** parameter WIDTH which will be ignored by the end user.

Regarding scheduling though, WIDTH is the dimension you will schedule/ keep track of. This ultimately is the actual WIDTH of our table. Let's illustrate.

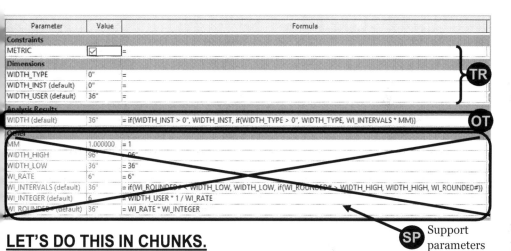

LET'S DO THIS IN CHUNKS.

① OUR TRIGGERS

Probably the easiest part of the formula and the only part the end user will concern themselves with. Our **triggers** consist of (4) parameters:

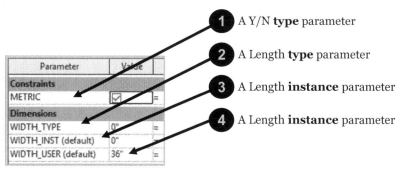

① A Y/N **type** parameter

② A Length **type** parameter

③ A Length **instance** parameter

④ A Length **instance** parameter

Note, instance parameters are easily identifiable by the **(default)** note next to them.

2 OUR OUTPUT PARAMETER WIDTH (INSTANCE LENGTH)

Our Elvis and his roadies (the rest of the **support** parameters and **triggers**). Our **output** parameter organizes all the **support** parameters acrobatics and the **trigger's** commands and pushes out the final WIDTH. Let's break it up.

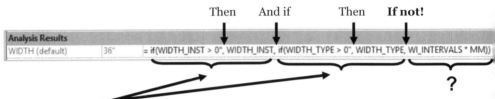

These two are easy, they are both just our **trigger** parameters which basically state: If WIDTH_INST is greater than 0" then whatever WIDTH_INST is will now be WIDTH, and If WIDTH_TYPE is greater than 0" then whatever WIDTH_TYPE is will now be WIDTH, **if not!**, then WIDTH will be **WI_INTERVALS*MM**. So lets now see what WI_INTERVALS is. **MM** has a whole section in the book, so we already know what it's doing here, turning WIDTH into metric. Thus, the last piece of the puzzle is... **WI_INTERVALS**.

RECAP

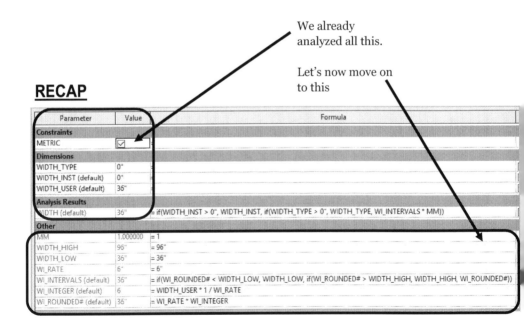

3 WIDTH_INTERVALS

SP WIDTH_INTERVALS is the **support** for WIDTH. Since it is doing all the heavy lifting (e.g., roadies), it gets messy, dirty, and downright unreplicable, but again, a formula like this **only needs to work once**, and you are set for tons of functionality. Follow below. We are going to focus on the parameters that start with WI_ since these are the main parameters that form WI_INTERVALS. That said, other participants help wrap up the formula, but we will discuss when we get there.

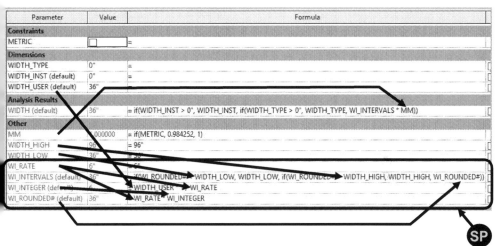

PARAMETER TYPES

Note, all the **support** parameters are Length parameters except **MM** and **WI_INTERVALS**. **MM** is a number parameter, and **WI_INTERVALS** is an integer parameter. Also, there are (3) instance parameters which are the parameters followed by (default). These are WI_INTERVALS, WI_INTEGER, and WI_ROUNDED.

Other		
MM	1.000000	= if(METRIC, 0.984252, 1)
WIDTH_HIGH	96"	= 96"
WIDTH_LOW	36"	= 36"
WI_RATE	6"	= 6"
WI_INTERVALS (default)	36"	= if(WI_ROUNDED# < WIDTH_LOW, WIDTH_LOW, if(WI_ROUNDED# > WIDTH_HIGH, WIDTH_HIGH, WI_ROUNDED#))
WI_INTEGER (default)	6	= WIDTH_USER * 1 / WI_RATE
WI_ROUNDED# (default)	36"	= WI_RATE * WI_INTEGER

WI PARAMETERS

Other		
MM	1.000000	= if(METRIC, 0.984252, 1)
WIDTH_HIGH	96"	= 96"
WIDTH_LOW	36"	= 36"
WI_RATE	6"	= 6"
WI_INTERVALS (default)	36"	= if(WI_ROUNDED# < WIDTH_LOW, WIDTH_LOW, if(WI_ROUNDED# > WIDTH_HIGH, WIDTH_HIGH, WI_ROUNDED#))
WI_INTEGER (default)	6	= WIDTH_USER * 1 / WI_RATE
WI_ROUNDED# (default)	36"	= WI_RATE * WI_INTEGER

WI_RATE (TYPE LENGTH)

This parameter sets the rate at which your table will grow, e.g., every 6". It could easily be changed to 3" or 12" increments.

WI_INTEGER (INSTANCE INTEGER)

This parameter takes the WIDTH_USER, or user input, and strips away the decimals, or any other mistake the user might have made, converting it into an **integer** which would eliminate any erroneous information. It then takes the rounded number, and by dividing it by the rate (WI_RATE), you get how many times the **rate** fits in the intended WIDTH. Note the *1 is there on purpose. Since you cannot use a Length parameter within integer parameters, by multiplying or dividing by (1) Revit accepts Length. See the "**Errors**" section on the back of the book for more on this. Just know for now that this is why it's there.

WI_ROUNDED# (INSTANCE LENGTH)

Up to now, all the work has been to achieve WI_ROUNDED#. This parameter's **output** is the 6" increment **output** we have been doing formula gymnastics for. Everything down from here (WI_INTERVALS and WIDTH) are really just organizing trigger data.

Now, by multiplying WI_RATE*WI_INTEGER, you get a perfectly rounded number in 3", 6", 12", or whatever increments you desire. Try it, make it, copy it.

Now, since this is really the critical parameter. I want you to analyze it at different intervals. I will also change the WIDTH_USER to 39" so it has more dynamic inputs.

AT WI_RATE = 3"

WIDTH_USER (default)	39"	=
Analysis Results		
WIDTH (default)	39"	= if(WIDTH_INST > 0", WIDTH_INST,
Other		
MM	1.000000	= if(METRIC, 0.984252, 1)
WIDTH_HIGH	96"	= 96"
WIDTH_LOW	36"	= 36"
WI_RATE	3"	= 3"
WI_INTERVALS (default)	39"	= if(WI_ROUNDED# < WIDTH_LOW,
WI_INTEGER (default)	13	= WIDTH_USER * 1 / WI_RATE
WI_ROUNDED# (default)	39"	= WI_RATE * WI_INTEGER

AT WI_RATE = 6"

WIDTH_USER (default)	39"	=
Analysis Results		
WIDTH (default)	42"	= if(WIDTH_INST > 0", WIDTH_INST,
Other		
MM	1.000000	= if(METRIC, 0.984252, 1)
WIDTH_HIGH	96"	= 96"
WIDTH_LOW	36"	= 36"
WI_RATE	6"	= 6"
WI_INTERVALS (default)	42"	= if(WI_ROUNDED# < WIDTH_LOW,
WI_INTEGER (default)	7	= WIDTH_USER * 1 / WI_RATE
WI_ROUNDED# (default)	42"	= WI_RATE * WI_INTEGER

AT WI_RATE = 12"

WIDTH_USER (default)	39"	=
Analysis Results		
WIDTH (default)	36"	= if(WIDTH_INST > 0", WIDTH_INST,
Other		
MM	1.000000	= if(METRIC, 0.984252, 1)
WIDTH_HIGH	96"	= 96"
WIDTH_LOW	36"	= 36"
WI_RATE	12"	= 12"
WI_INTERVALS (default)	36"	= if(WI_ROUNDED# < WIDTH_LOW,
WI_INTEGER (default)	3	= WIDTH_USER * 1 / WI_RATE
WI_ROUNDED# (default)	36"	= WI_RATE * WI_INTEGER

WI_INTERVALS (INSTANCE INTEGER)

So, we now have a parameter (WI_ROUNDED#) that will **output** a WIDTH from 0" to infinite " at 6" increments or whatever you decide. Now, the final piece of the puzzle, making stops at 36" for the low end and 96" for the high end. That is what this parameter/ formula does.

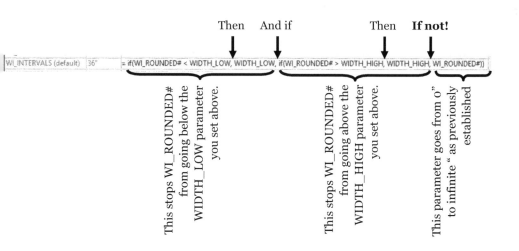

FINAL THOUGHTS

It looks like a lot of information to untangle in this formula but just use it, copy it, change the parameter names to suit your needs and run with it. With time you can come back and further analyze it or use some of its principles on another formula you may be developing.

When broken down it does look like a lot but we really just wanted to show how these come together in **chunks**.

When you are set on developing a new capability, you begin with writing what you want in English. As you hit every point, it organically goes like this in sections, in **chunks**. Later you may come back and add more capabilities or subtract, but the process goes in **chunks**.

In this formula, the hardest **chunk** was to get the parameter to grow in intervals we could control. All the other capabilities are pretty easy to come up with. Capabilities like these sometimes take time, but as you get better and are exposed to other complex formulas, it will become second nature.

Note, if you can add a formula like this to a pull, guess what? You don't even have to type in numbers. You just pull on the graphic, and it jumps to the next interval and the next interval. Oh, and you can use the **align tool** with pulls for speedier changes. **Hint**.

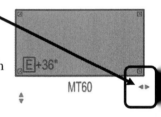

Play with your component.

These pulls are generated when you use instance parameters. Type parameters do not develop pulls. You can also use **reference lines** for the pull. This lets you further control where the pull is placed. That's how we got the pull perfectly in front of the table in this example. Setting a reference plane to **not a reference** eliminates the pull's graphic when using instance parameters. Play around with this, you can really make some cool stuff.

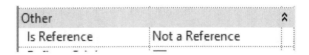

INTENTIONAL BREAK

TEXT FORMULAS

Text parameters can be used for anything, from communicating notes to future you, to sorting families by a word or words through a schedule.

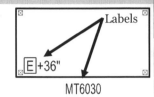

The primary uses I found for text parameters are:

- For **Keynoting** families.

- And in **labels**.

See labels above on example MT. Labels can connect to Length parameters, e.g., the 6030 for WIDTH and DEPT, and the +36" for HEIGHT. Additionally, it can connect to Material parameters (E, for epoxy), and of course, **Text parameters** (the MT in MT6030). The Revit label is not just dumb text. The Revit label is a powerful family in its own right.

Additional to keynoting and communicating 3D data in a 2D plan, text parameters **can be used in formulas!** For what? Well, let's explore and illustrate.

EASY BASICS

With text it's straightforward, you have (3) options:

1. You fill the value field, and you're done.
2. You Gray the value empty with (2) quotation marks, " ".
3. You gray the value with permanent text by putting the text between (2) quotation marks, e.g., "TEXT_GRAY".

Parameter	Value	Formula
Text		
TEXT_PRMTR_A		=
TEXT_PRMTR_B	TEXT_GRAY	= "TEXT_GRAY"

It is that easy. Now let's see what we can do with these simple rules.

'G' MOVABLE BASE CABINET LABEL

Let's introduce a new family, the 'G' movable base cabinet. This cabinet has a smart label (or a regular Revit label used smartly), which reacts to 3D/Y/N parameters to inform the user as to what is going on in 3D via the Label. See below, this cabinet is either on CASTERS or on GLIDES. Has either a LOCK or a HASP. These (2) "eithers" is what our formulas will center on.

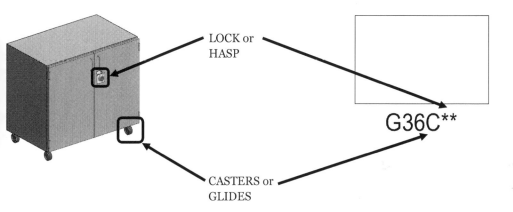

A BIT MORE ON THE LABEL

The movable base cabinet label consists of (3) parts. The name of the cabinet 'G,' the WIDTH of the cabinet 36", and the SUFFIX. The SUFFIX **outputs** the cabinet's LOCK, HASP, CASTERS, GLIDES, or a combination of the (4). The only thing it cannot have is a LOCK and a HASP at the same time, or a CASTER and a GLIDE at the same time. In real life, you wouldn't order a cabinet on CASTERS and GLIDES. So, how do we protect our selves from this ERROR? Well, let's have the family tell us there is an ERROR.

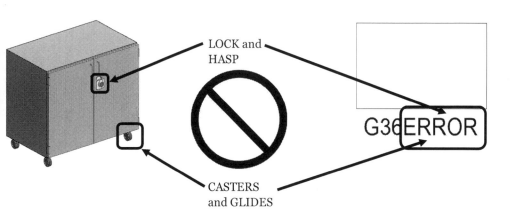

SUFFIX PLAN

Now, we want a SUFFIX text parameter that will output all listed below **triggered** by (4) Y/N parameters, CASTERS, GLIDES, LOCK, and HASP:

LABEL	SUFFIX MEANING
G36	NO SUFFIX (EMPTY)
G36*	LOCK
G36**	HASP
G36C	CASTERS
G36G	GLIDES
G36C*	CASTERS AND LOCK
G36C**	CASTERS AND HASP
G36G*	GLIDES AND LOCK
G36G**	GLIDES AND HASP

FORMULA

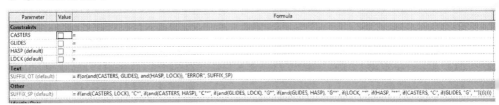

THE BREAKDOWN

Here is our basic layout. **Triggers**, **output** and **support** parameters.

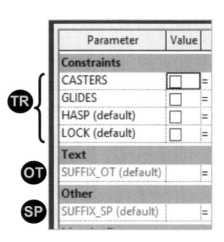

SP SUPPORT PARAMETER

Note, I really split this formula in two. The reality is, this formula could have easily been one continuous horizontal formula, but perhaps it's best to break it in two for clarity.

In this case, the **support** parameter formula will **output** all the combinations we organized and listed on the suffix plan. The **resting** text (end of formula) will be empty ("").

Note as well that the order from left to right matters. You want the more complicated combinations to the right, and the simpler single Y/N clicks to the left to get this formula to work.

This formula is a perfect example of just how infinite and powerful the If( ) function can be. It is a basic If( ) function with some And ( ) functions in the middle.

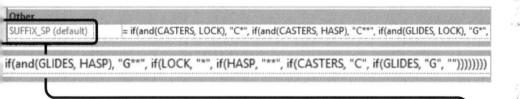

OT OUTPUT PARAMETER - ERROR MESSAGE

This parameter is more straightforward than it looks. Like most **OT** parameters, it's just acting as the organizer for all the **support** and **trigger** parameters to **output** a finished product with the added formula to signal **ERROR!**

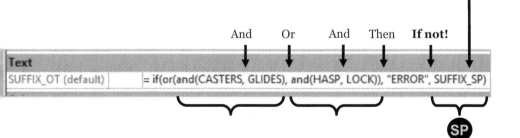

PART 5

SOME 'BEFORE YOU GO' TOPICS THAT WERE HARD TO BRING UP UNTIL THE END. THINGS THAT MAY HAVE CAUSED CONFUSION, BUT NOW YOU ARE READY.

POST-PARAMETERS AND FORMULAS

PARAMETER ORGANIZING

Now that you've seen how long and tall formula structure can get, perhaps you're beginning to think of how to better organize all those trigger, output, text, and support parameters. The solution to organizing parameters is altering how they are **grouped**.

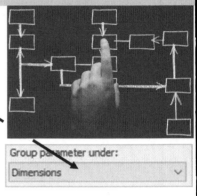

Up to now, you are used to Revit grouping your parameters for you, e.g., Length goes to Dimensions, and text to Text, etc., but it does not have to be this way. You can take **control** of your groups, all you need is a plan. I'll let you borrow mine, though it is open to change of course. So you be you.

Now you may be thinking, why is this not under the parameters section? Well, this is because you weren't ready, you were a **newb!** And I get it, I was one once too. You can't begin to think of organizing dozens of parameters if you haven't seen why you would need to organize dozens of parameters. You had to see long formulas for that **aha moment**. So, that's why it's here. OK, got it, good, let's go.

In general, we need to organize an distribute (3) **chunks** of data:

INPUT/TRIGGER PARAMETERS	OUTPUT PARAMETERS	SUPPORT PARAMETERS
(Can be more than one) **TR**	(Can only be one) **OT**	(Can be more than one) **SP**

NO NEED TO ORGANIZE THESE PARAMETERS

There will be some parameters that do not need to be lumped into these (3) categories. Letting them sit in their default groups will suffice. These parameters are the non-formulable parameters discussed at the beginning of the book:

- URL
- Material
- Image
- <family type...>

INTENTIONAL BREAK

DIAGRAM VS. REAL LIFE

Let's circle back to the **"anatomy of a formula part deux'** section under the **formula ideas** part. Look at the diagram below, and then the parameters and groups on the next sheet. The parameters, formulas and the family is not important. What is important is the **organization**. Look back and forth. With little explanation, you can see the way I organize my parameters is a direct correlation to how formulas work. Think of this part as the **IOS** analogy. We want to bury all the confusing parameters and formulas we used to make our complex families and provide the end user with a clean, easy to reach set of controls (**triggers**) they can just click and go. So, to that end, **triggers** are always placed on top, and the remaining parameters fall below. They are grayed out and out of the way. How is this hierarchy achieved? By using select groups that stack properly. See below how the **chunks** are organized.

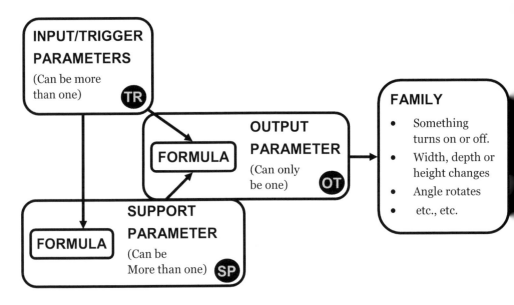

TR TRIGGER CHUNK

Triggers are the most crucial part of organizing parameters. This **chunk** is really the only part the end user will care about. The rest is for you, the builder. I force all my **triggers** under the **Constraint** group **except** for of a handful of parameters. I'll discuss these shortly. The parameters you group under **Constraints** are Y/N & Integer parameters, since these account for 90% of what users will **trigger**. Also grouped here, and with less frequency, are the angle, number, and other less used **trigger** parameters. **So, who doesn't go here?** Length, Text, and of course parameters that cannot be used in formulas. Like materials. Why do I separate these two? Well, because they too account for a significant number of **trigger** parameters, but mostly because their group's Length & Text already suit them perfectly and the end user will appreciate them labeled separately.

While the **Constraint** group may not have been intended for this purpose, it does always guarantee that your **trigger** parameters end up on top, and that is very, very, important. The end user will not care that you have parameters placed in the **Constraint** section. The end user wants to go in and out fast. Period.

OT) OUTPUT CHUNK

For the output chunk, I like the **Analysis Results** group. The **Analysis results** group falls right under the aforementioned groups including the Text group, and it literally has the word **results** in it, which is a very accurate description of the output parameters. Here I don't discriminate parameters, I lump all Y/N, Integer, Length, Text, etc. in one. Why? Because it lets me come back and see what is connected to the family easily in one section, plus, the **trigger** section is meant for the end user's clarity, not mine. I am used to all this **gobbly goop**, and I can handle it. The end users need his Length parameters nicely under **Dimensions**, the Text under **Text**, etc.

SP) SUPPORT CHUNK

The remaining parameters are easily lumped under **Other**. Again, these are the least important to the end user, and maybe even you. The **Other** group drags them all the way to the bottom, or pretty close to the bottom. Out of sight and out of mind.

Parameter	Value	Formula
Constraints		
LASER_CURTAIN	☐	=
CURTAIN (default)	☑	=
ANGLE_FLIP (default)	☐	=
ANGLE (default)	0.000°	=
Materials and Finishes		
MATERIAL	TOEKICK	=
Dimensions		
WIDTH (default)	60"	=
SKIRT_HEIGHT	12"	=
RADIUS	12"	=
DEPTH	2"	=
CURTAIN_THICKNESS	1/4"	=
CEILING_HEIGHT	108"	=
Analysis Results		
STRAIGHT_SKIRT_VIS (default)	☑	= not(ANGLE > 0°)
SKIRT_HEIGHT_USED	-12"	= SKIRT_HEIGHT * FLIP
LASER_CURTAIN_USED (default)	☐	= if(not(CURTAIN), OFF, LASER_CURTAIN)
BLACKOUT_CURTAIN (default)	☑	= if(not(CURTAIN), OFF, not(LASER_CURTAIN))
ANGLE_USED (default)	90.000°	= if(ANGLE > 0°, ANGLE, 90°)
ANGLE2_VIS (default)	☐	= and(ANGLE > 0°, not(ANGLE_FLIP))
ANGLE1_VIS (default)	☐	= and(ANGLE > 0°, ANGLE_FLIP)
Other		
ON	☑	= 0 + 0 = 0
OFF	☐	= 0 + 0 = 1
FLIP	-1.000000	= -1
Identity Data		
KEYNOTE	TBD	=
Type Image		=

KISS - THOUGHTS

There is no right or wrong way to go about it, just have a strategy that works for you. This (3) **chunk** strategy has been tried and true for me, and I recommend you borrow it until you come up with your own.

I have also at times used the **Title Text** group for example, as my support parameter area for making text formulas. Therefore separating text complexity from **Other**. Since it has the word text, mentally it helps me lump them together.

I have also used the **Data** group and the **Structural Analysis** groups if a particular output parameter requires too many support parameters and formulas. This helps me lump data for just (1) **output** parameter. Again this is up to you. I only go this route if it gets too messy otherwise, **KISS!** Keep it simple s!@#$%.

Have fun.

INTENTIONAL BREAK

COMMON ERRORS

Errors. The worst. Here is a list of common errors you will encounter, their causes, and their solutions. For the most part, errors often occur for very straightforward reasons, e.g., you forgot a capital letter, misspelled a parameter's name, or forgot to add an end parentheses ').' Don't panic, there is often a solution to your error unless you are trying to do something which is impossible, like make a formula with a material. Not gonna happen. See below and look for what is ailing you.

MISSPELL

This error occurs when you don't write a parameter name correctly in a formula. In this case, we are missing the 'D' for WIDTH, or the original is Width (case sensitivity). Merely verify you are writing the initial parameter correctly.

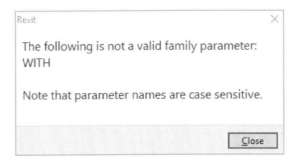

CIRCULAR CHAIN

This error occurs when you write a formula in your trigger parameter. In other words, you try writing a formula in the same parameter that will trigger said formula.

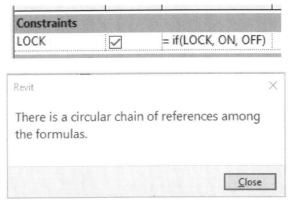

TO MANY PARENTHESIS

This error occurs when you add more parenthesis that are needed, e.g., if (WIDTH>30",ON,OFF)). In this If( ) formula there is one to many parenthesis.

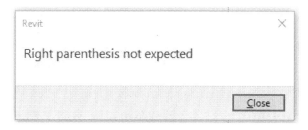

TO FEW PARENTHESIS

This error is the opposite of the one above. This occurs when you need to add one or more parenthesis to finish your formula, e.g., if(WIDTH>30",ON,OFF. In this If ( ) formula you need to close the formula with a final parenthesis.

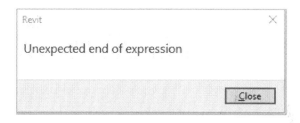

INCOMPLETE IF STATEMENT

This error occurs when you haven't finished your if ( ) formula correctly, e.g., if(WIDTH>30",ON). In this example, we need to add what happens when WIDTH is not greater than 30" to finish the formula correctly.

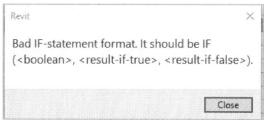

INSTANCE WILL NOT OVERRIDE A TYPE

Instance parameters are weaker than type parameters. When this happens, make sure that all your parameters are Instance parameters if your **trigger** is an instance parameter. If your **trigger** is a type parameter, you should not get this error. The type parameter is stronger than an instance parameter.

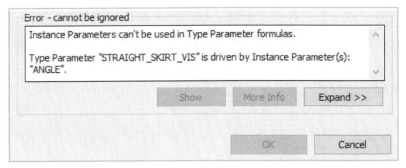

INCONSISTENT UNITS

By far the **WORST** of all the errors. This can happen when you **trigger** parameters are different unit types than your **output** parameter. Let me illustrate, but before all that, let me give you the solution up front. This can be neutralized by **dividing** a parameter by **one** or **multiplying** by **one**. Period. Now let's illustrate:

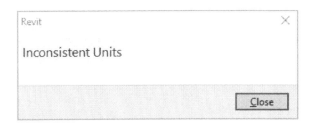

Here we have (3) parameters. (2) Length parameters under **Dimensions** and (1) integer parameter under **Analysis Results.**

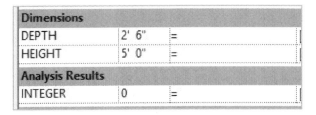

Now, what I want to do is multiply DEPTH * HEIGHT, and whatever the result is have it automatically converted to an integer. Let's try it. Result, ERROR.

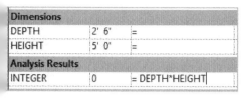 

Neutralize it. By merely dividing one of the Length parameters by one, the formula works, and the resultant 12.5 gets rounded to the nearest integer 13.

Dimensions		
DEPTH	2' 6"	=
HEIGHT	5' 0"	=
Analysis Results		
INTEGER	13	= DEPTH * (HEIGHT / 1 SF)

This happened before when we were making our WI_INTEGER formula in the next level formula section. Just know that the solution is either PARAMETER/1 or PARAMETER*1.

WI_INTEGER (default)	10	= TOGGLE_WIDTH * 1 / WI_RATE

HERE IS AUTODESK'S EXPLANATION, BUT THE SOLUTION IS THE SAME:

Causes:

The units are inconsistent. This can happen when units have become unbalanced, for example:

10 mm * 10 mm = 100 mm^2

Solution:

Balance the units within the equation. To correctly get 100 mm, the equation would have to look like:
10 mm * (10 mm / 1 mm) = 100 mm

Why? Because <100 mm / 1 mm = 100> (unit less) and <100 mm * 100 = 10,000 mm>

TIPS AND TRICKS

Many of the tips and tricks noted here are scattered throughout the book. They are marked by the word **Hint** at the end of the tip. Though, I thought it would be helpful to corral them in this section for further clarity.

- **CHANGING MATERIALS ON THE FLY.**

    If you know the material name, you can just type it, and Revit will find it for you. There is no need to go through the materials properties box and scroll through a giant list of materials to find one. In fact, if you are changing a couple of materials frequently, make their names really simple, e.g., Epoxy = EP, or Wood = WO. This way you just type the first (2) letters and you are done.

- **PARENTHESIS-END IN EMBEDDED IF STATEMENTS - IF(A,IF(B,C,D))**

    In conditional If( ) formulas, when you embed multiple if( ) functions, the amount of if( ) functions directly correlates to the number of parentheses at the end. See the example below.

    If(A, if(B, if(C, D, E)))

    You see, there are (3) If functions, which means you need (3) parentheses to close the formula. This is an error that comes up often. Simply knowing this will take some pressure off. If the formula is long and complex, I often add extra parentheses and delete one by one until the formula takes. **Hint.**

- **PARAMETER STRENGTH FROM LEFT TO RIGHT**

    Revit reads parameters from left to right. What this means is that in an embedded IF( ) statement like the one above, the statement to the left will be triggered before the ones to the right. Another way to see this is that the statement to the left **is stronger** than the one to the right.

- **WRITE YOUR PARAMETERS IN ENGLISH FIRST**

    When planning your parameters and formulas, always write them down in plain English first. This helps you organize your thoughts before you even hit Revit. Once in English, then try to write down what you need (parameter types) to make your formula. Then try writing your plan with conditional statements. You will quickly see that planning things out first will buy you time and avoid headaches in the family editor.

INTENTIONAL BREAK

FINAL THOUGHTS

I suppose that if you are reading this, you made it through. If you just skipped to the end well... that's fine too. In fact, it is encouraged. Since the beginning, we've invited the reader to explore through the book. To seek and find what got you to buy the book, and run with it. In learning, there is no right or wrong, only **growth**.

I firmly believe that if you've read through the book, you are now miles ahead of where I was when I began making components. If you doubt for a minute that you can put any of it's material to use **DON'T**. Just use what you need as you need it, and with time you will find that:

A. Many examples translate directly to everyday tasks you're doing.

B. You eventually will come up with your own version of similar formulas.

If it looks daunting, remember that it literally took years to assemble all this data, so don't expect to use it, or digest it all in a week. If you can, go for it.

The idea is that you're **exposed** to the information. Sometimes exposure is more important than memorizing content because, with exposure, you don't need to memorize; just remember. When you remember, you can just reach out to the book on your bookshelf, and extract the information. Memorization comes with practice. Learn by doing.

Take this knowledge, and use it to advance. I know it progressed me tremendously, and I am happy to have shared it with you.

Sincerely.

Edgar E.B.
NCARB

THE REVIT® FORMULA

To **learn** more about this book, and upcoming material, visit us at:

www.TheRevitFormula.com

If you would like to share insights, ideas, or if you have questions

reach out by email at:

www.ContactUs@TheRevitFormula.com

To order more copies, check our website for platform details.

Thanks for your interest, and we wish you **great success**.

DEDICATION DEDICATION DEDICATION DEDICATION

TO MY WIFE WHO'S TRUST, FRIENDSHIP, AND CONFIDENCE FEED MY PASSION THROUGH THIS LIFE TOGETHER

TO MY BEAUTIFUL DAUGHTER WHO HELPS ME KEEP MY CHILD LIKE AMBITION MOVING IN AN ENERGETIC FUN DIRECTION; MY HEART.

Made in the USA
Monee, IL
21 January 2022